Preface

An introduction to **ARROJO**

01

Many people who have picked up this book will have done so because they know the name Nick Arrojo from the television show What Not to Wear. Indeed, the book is all about me helping women with their own hair journey, just like I do on the show. But in this special preface, I also want to give you a short introduction to ARROJO, a fantastic team committed to hairdressing excellence.

02

In the beginning, ARROJO studio was a hair salon with six chairs and five members of staff. The idea was to use terrific service and quality hairdressing to make sure each client left our salon looking and feeling like a million dollars. What I did and what I encouraged my staff to do was educate the client about their hair. To talk about what works and what doesn't, to explain how to incorporate a new trend, to explain how to style and finish the look. My commitment, and the commitment of the salon, was to share our experience and expertise to help people achieve successful hairstyles. Today, the salon has grown to include forty stylists and many support staff, but the belief in sharing insights about hair remains the same.

03

04

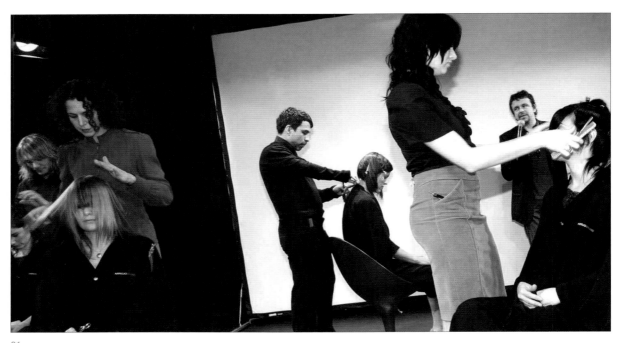

01

As the company grew, this philosophy became integral to other things that we do. In the same way we believed in education for the client, we believed we could inspire and educate other hairdressers, too. The conviction was that by teaching other hairdressers to be more creative, inspired, technically precise, and professional, we'd be shaping a stronger, more dynamic industry, one that would be more able to make each person that sits in a hairdressers' chair look and feel terrific.

01. The ARROJO education team onstage at a New York City show.

02. The arrojoproduct.com Web home page.

03. Showing information about one of our seminars, a Web page from arrojoeducation.com.

04. Our first full-color newsletter, released in spring 2006.

05. A brochure for the ARROJO academy, where our educational seminars take place.

It's also true that the best way to become a better stylist is to teach. In teaching others, you have to talk and think about hair, and that helps us improve our game as well. Education began as one or two seminars a year in our salon space. Now my team and I teach at hair and beauty shows and seminars across America. The goal is to give fellow hairdressers insights to how we work. To provide advanced, inspirational and career-shaping education that is usable every day with clients on the salon floor. But the reason why education was formed in the first place funnels back to the original idea of the salon: that our knowledge, experience, and expertise is worth sharing.

With the success of the salon and education, we developed two Web sites, arrojostudio.com and arrojoeducation.com. These sites have become a critical part of our business because they share our content and identity with the world. Each Web site displays content specific to that part of the company and, through the images and information, can offer a great idea of who we are and what we're about. The design is elegant, eye-catching, functional, and modern, the copy fuss-free and direct––elements easily found in the hairstyles created in the salon and in the teaching philosophy of our education. It underscores that everything the company does begins from the same ideas and values.

With many thousands of visits each month, the Web sites proved people were interested in knowing more about us. We started making our own newsletters with information about salon promotions, latest trends, and show and seminar reports, and we gave one to each client. It was the first time we had produced our own printed matter; it was very much aligned with our philosophy of sharing our identity and information.

02

03

04

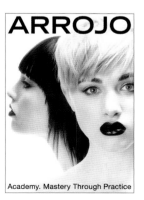

05

The newsletters then gave way to the ARROJO magazine, produced, written, and designed in-house by the team. Moving to a magazine gave us more room to breathe: now we could include editorial collections and articles about the salon, education, and the people behind the chair. In many ways, the idea was similar to this preface. For example, a salon client might not know too much about how we teach hairdressers all around the world, but from an article in our magazine they can see how much respect the company has inside the industry. Another client might be thinking about trying a new look. Through our editorial collections that feature in the magazine, maybe she'll find the piece of inspiration she's looking for. Then she can go to her stylist and say, "I love this look. How can you make it work for me"? It all relates to going the extra mile, as we did when we first opened the salon. We just have more tools at our disposal now.

Speaking of tools, the next step for us was to create our own hair care line. The product concept was simple: luxury with performance. It had to match ARROJO studio's hairdressers' expectations of product performance; and, being a beauty product, it had to look, feel, and work like one. Today the commitment is to a professional standard product available to everyone. It's a commitment we ourselves fulfill through arrojoproduct.com, our e-commerce Web site. And with styling tips and advice (direct from ARROJO studio stylists) that helps each person get the most performance and styling flexibility out of each product, the Web site is another example of how we love to share hairstyling know-how.

01

02

01. Following on from the newsletters, ARROJO magazine 1 makes our print media more professional.

02. ARROJO magazine 2 shares new content, new editorials, and new inspiration.

03. ARROJO product, conceptualized, designed, and promoted in-house.

Nowadays, ARROJO is an independent, contemporary hairdressing brand dedicated to hair salon services, hairdressing education for the professional and for the client, and professional hair products and tools for everyone. I truly believe we got to this point by being willing and open enough to share our insights, ideas, and inspirations with the client, with our peers, and, through print and Web media, with anyone anywhere in the world who is interested in the things we do.

I feel it is important to note that it's more than just me who is committed to Great Hair. Many people ask, "How do you do what you do"? But, really, it's not just me. Any hairdresser committed to the craft of hairdressing, and committed to communicating with the client for their successful hairstyle, can do the things that I do. I know because I see a team of stylists doing them every day. It was the success of my original philosophy that gave me the belief a book like this would be a positive and valuable asset for women. I find it happily appropriate that the book's content says many of the things I, and the team of stylists I work with, say to people each day.

Great
Hair

Nick Arrojo

Great Hair

Secrets to Looking Fabulous
and Feeling Beautiful Every Day

Photographs by Jenny Acheson

St. Martin's Griffin ⚜ New York

Book design by Ralph Fowler / rlf design
Production manager: Adriana Coada

ISBN-13: 978-0-312-55557-3
ISBN-10: 0-312-55557-1

First Edition: October 2008

10 9 8 7 6 5 4 3 2 1

To clients and
hairdressers alike:
I hope this book
inspires you to make
Great Hair a passionate
and enjoyable part of
your life, each and
every day.

Contents

Introduction

When I was growing up just outside
Manchester, England, I was constantly

re-creating my image. Completely inspired by music and fashion, I
spent every day of my teenage years reading the key fashion magazines
of the time (of which there were very few) and getting into all the new
trends. My older brother was a hair colorist at one of the best salons in
Manchester, and he was the coolest and hippest person I knew. He
changed his style frequently, and he inspired me to do the same.

Although my clothes would change, it was difficult for me to change
my hair because I had some insecurities about my looks. My sticking-
out ears and high forehead made me determined to keep my hair long
to cover up these so-called failings. I didn't like my hair's curliness much,
either. On the one occasion I cut and straightened my hair, the results
were disastrous and embarrassing.

I suppose it was inevitable that I became a hairdresser. At first, I just
thought a hair salon would be a great environment in which to work, that
I'd get to meet lots of new and interesting people and have the chance
to be creatively involved in the fashion industry. Besides, I needed a
job—and some spending money—to help me enjoy those teenage
years. At sixteen, I landed my first job and became a hair assistant at
the biggest salon in Bolton, a town just up the road from where I lived.

I loved my new job straightaway. There was a hip young staff, music playing all day, friendly clients, lots of energy, and parties every weekend. How could I not love it? I realized pretty quickly that I wanted hairdressing to be my career. I also realized that if I was going to do this for the rest of my life, I wanted to be great at it. Now I had to work out how to be the best that I could be and make it to the top of my industry.

I was sure that I needed the best education possible in order to have a chance of making it big, so I went to the Big City: Manchester. By luck or by fate, I landed a job at the best salon in the country, Vidal Sassoon.

Vidal Sassoon was located in an iconic five-story building on famous King Street, Manchester's fashionable epicenter, complete with cobblestones and dainty trees. With its brown-tinted windows and larger-than-life images of amazing cuts and colors hanging throughout the majestic and futuristic space, Vidal Sassoon had an intimidating presence that reminded me of ultrahip London. I had arrived at the real deal, the place of excellence that was all things hair and all things cool. Vidal had revolutionized the hair industry with his precision-based technique, and now I was one of his new disciples.

I soon realized that I lacked true natural ability, but I vowed not to let that stand in my way. I would just have to work harder. And I did. Every day, I was the first in and the last to leave. I wanted to make a name for myself and build a reputation that would earn me the respect of my peers. I attended every single training class and gave 100 percent toward improving my skills.

I learned from my mistakes and observed carefully, striving to be the best.

Once my apprenticeship was over, I became a stylist, and two years later, I was promoted to assistant creative director at the Manchester salon. I was just twenty-one then and I had already learned a lot. I learned that hair is an accessory to your total image. I learned that if you work with your hair in its natural state you will achieve greater success in maintaining your style. I learned that a precision cut is the most fundamentally important thing. I learned that my skills were getting better and better as my experience grew. And I learned that I was slowly overcoming my insecurities about my own hair, forehead, and ears.

With this newfound confidence, I began encouraging clients to change their opinions about their hair. I wanted them to work with their hair in a more natural, easy way, but I was faced with many people who had their own insecurities to contend with. I realized that if I was going to counsel people to look past their issues to see what the possibilities were, then I had to banish my own insecurities for good. After all, how could I give advice that I wasn't willing to take myself?

I liberated myself by shaving my head. Without the long bangs I'd been hiding behind, my forehead and stick-out ears were completely exposed. This was my lesson to myself, and do you know what? It really helped! Nobody else seemed to mind what I thought were my odd features. I experienced and overcame my insecurities. Change was good!

I continued to evolve as a stylist and I

continued to love my work. I helped people to become ecstatic about the way they look every day, and I still love the feeling I get from sharing that moment with them. Whenever I get the chance to see a new client, someone lost in her own hair dilemma, I gladly take it. I believe I have the confidence and the skill to lead people toward a whole new perspective about themselves, and when they get there and can finally see themselves as I do, it's like magic. It gives me a great sense of personal satisfaction every time.

I moved to New York City in 1994. It was a dream fully realized and a fantasy come true to live in the Big Apple. As education director for a major New York City salon, I began formally educating other hairdressers. I loved, and continue to love, this part of my job. To pass on my experience to the next generation of stylists and help them to become true masters of their craft is a real honor. It's why I recently opened my own academy for advanced hairdressing education.

After living in New York for eight years, I was lucky enough to be asked to show my skills on the television show *What Not to Wear*. It was around that time that I began thinking about how great it would be to educate not just hairdressers but clients as well. I thought that with the right education and understanding about their hair, clients would have a better chance of maintaining a great hairstyle and be loads happier.

Those thoughts continued to percolate while I became somewhat of a hair celebrity. The TV experience helped me grow even more as a

stylist. When I watch the show, I can witness and reflect on what it is we do for the client. I've learned from watching my own chairside manner and by seeing how the client likes to wear her hair after she has left the salon. I get a sense of how she really feels about the experience, and most important, whether I was right about what she needed and whether I helped her. Then it hit me: In order for hairstylists to grow and improve, we *must* educate our clients. We have to help them understand more about their potential.

I see so many clients with the same problems, problems they think are unique to them but really aren't. Maybe they have had bad advice in the past and that has scarred or tainted them. Maybe they just have the wrong perspective and need to be shown the true nature of their hair and what it can and can't do. I have met and successfully styled tens of thousands of clients, and with all my knowledge and experience, and with my newfound visibility, I truly believe now is the time to put all this information into one concise, thorough, and—I hope—enlightening book.

The ideas, thoughts, and opinions that I want to share with you will give you the information you need to achieve something that is important to all women: fantastic, attainable, and easy-to-wear Great Hair. I want to dispel all the myths and help everyone see the realities so they can feel great about their hair and themselves. My goal is not only to help everyone to rethink their hairstyle and styling choices, but also to prove that if you work with your hair in a natural way, you will, without question, achieve a fantastic look.

This book can be used in two ways. Read it from start to finish for a completely new perspective on every aspect of hair, or pick and choose the sections that relate most to you. I also suggest that you keep this book by your vanity mirror and use my how-to styling sections anytime you want to shape and style your hair. I encourage everyone to start with a clean slate and an open mind because this could be the wake-up call your hair has been waiting for, and it may just dispel many of your preconceived ideas about hair.

I will begin by showing you how to understand and care for the hair you have. Then I hope to inspire you to make some changes for the better. No matter what kind of hair you have—whether it's curly or straight, thick or thin, dark or light, or somewhere in between—this book presents lots of options so that the new hairstyle you choose will also suit who you are. Chapter 3, "The Ultimate Hairstyle Guide," has all sorts of different styles for you to choose from. All the women in this style guide (and in the makeover section of the book) are real women from age fifteen to fifty who applied to be part of this project through an advertisement on my salon Web site. These aren't models who came to me with practically perfect hair. They are women who showed up in my salon carrying with them a whole range of issues and insecurities that they needed help with, just like you. *And* all the styles I created for them can be easily worn from day to day, or shaped into a magical special occasion do. I show real women in this book to prove to you that getting a great hairstyle, one that makes you look young, fresh, and more modern, is achievable for women of any age and any hair type.

Great Hair will also equip you with the information you need to find a great hairdresser and coach you on the right way to approach a consultation, a critical part of getting a hairstyle you love. I also show you how to style your hair and achieve different looks at home. Whether you want curls, or volume, or smoothness, and whether you want to use your fingers, a blow-dryer, or a hot iron to get the look, I show you how to make hairstyling creative, fun, and successful, whether it's for every day or a special occasion.

I take a close look at color and how it can beautifully enhance the way you look. I cover problem hair and maintenance and I give you salon secrets that are used to overcome common challenges. And because ethnic hair types come with their own unique set of assets and challenges, I devote an entire chapter to the different options and techniques available to women with this kind of hair.

In this book you'll find my voice, my vision, and all of the advice that I happily share with anyone who seeks me out, sits in my chair, and asks me for help. I believe everyone has the potential to achieve Great Hair. My prescription for making that happen for all types of hair and all kinds of women is all here and explained in a way that is easy to understand. Ultimately, I truly believe it's not just about how you look; it's about how your look makes you feel about yourself. I hope this book inspires you to be confident and beautiful, sexy and happy!

Great Hair

1. Getting to Know Your Hair

Every day in my hair salon, women ask me to give them a haircut that is the perfect fit for their face. They're sick and tired of having a haircut that doesn't suit them, and because it doesn't suit them, they spend an hour in the morning furiously trying to make it right—and failing. Just the other day, a lady having a consultation with me was convinced the shorter, more layered haircut I wanted to give her just wouldn't suit her face, which was marginally rounded. She was sure she needed to keep her hair long, and, in fact, was close to running out of the salon. She seemed to think this was the only way to save the life of her dated hairstyle. I explained to her that a great haircut gives you beautiful face-framing shape and complements your features perfectly. *But* the best way to do that is to get a cut that matches the texture and shape of your hair, not the shape of your face. Going for a low-maintenance hairstyle that works with—rather than against—your natural texture and shape makes you look fresh and modern, and it is easy for you to shape and style your hair each and every day. That's the message I give my clients and the message this book has for you.

Not every hairstyle suits every type of hair. If you choose from a range of hairstyles that match your own hair texture and shape, there will be no more fighting with your hair, no more running battles as you try to get out of the door on time in the morning, and no more spending lots of cash on the latest trendy styles that your hair just can't handle. Instead, understand your hair texture and shape first, and then pick hairstyles to match. Not only will the style suit you better, but when you truly know your own hair type, you can choose styling techniques, products, and tools that are your perfect match, too. Knowing and playing to the strengths of your hair type allow you to create modern, sexy, and healthy no-fuss hair—and who doesn't want that?

The lady who nearly ran from my chair understood what I could do for her, and,

thankfully, she decided to stay. She had fine, fragile, long hair when she came to me. I talk about this more as I progress, but for now, fine hair is more limp and lifeless—it has less natural volume and bounce—than thicker hair types, so wearing it long only accentuated how thin and weak her hair was. As a result, that nice lady was battling with her hair every morning as she tried to give it more structure and style. Even for the best stylists this would have been a serious challenge, if not nigh on impossible. So I gave her a midlength cut with lots and lots of layers and a much softer shape, which naturally gave her hair more lift, volume, and structure. She left the salon positively gleaming, looking fresh,

young, and modern. She looked that way because she had a soft-shaped haircut that suited her hair texture—not because I'd magically procured some perfect one-of-a-kind hairstyle for her very slightly rounded face. Day-to-day styling was made totally easy because she no longer had to try to create shape with long, flat, and lifeless hair.

I want the same thing for you. I want you to choose a hairstyle that matches your texture and shape, and then use the styling techniques, products, and tools that are right for you and your hair (all of which are discussed later in this book). That way you can play to your strengths, which will make you look youthful and contemporary—and all because you did the right things for your hair type!

The first step on your Great Hair journey is to figure out your hair's natural texture and shape. Let's tackle that right now.

Know Your Hair

After twenty-five years behind a salon chair, I can tell somebody's hair texture and shape within thirty seconds, but for you it may be a bit trickier. Hair is, after all, quite difficult to define because it is as unique as a fingerprint. Your hair could be straight, but the texture could be fine or thick or somewhere in between ("in between" is commonly referred to as "medium-smooth" hair texture). Or it could be a curly shape and still be fine, thick, or medium-smooth in texture. And that's not even taking into consideration the

> Fine hair is more limp and lifeless . . . than thicker hair types, so wearing it long only accentuated how thin and weak her hair was.

density of your hair—how many hairs you have on your head—which could be heavy, medium, or light. In other words, no matter what your hair's texture (fine, medium-smooth, coarse) and shape (straight, wavy, curly), there's the potential to have loads of hair or to have a light head of hair. There's a lot of variation. Let's simplify hair type by breaking down the different textures and shapes. Density doesn't have as much of an impact on which styles, products, and techniques you choose, but it does highlight how unique your hair really is.

Here's how to know your hair: Give it a good shampoo and condition, and then let it dry slowly and naturally. Every ten minutes or so, gently squeeze your hair in your hands. This helps bring out any natural wave or curl. The best time to examine your hair is when it's completely dry. Get up close and personal with

your mirror, and as you read the following sections, spend some time playing with and looking closely at your hair so you can get to know it as well as possible.

HAIR TEXTURE

Texture has to do with the diameter or thickness of the hair shaft, but if you don't work with all types of hair every day, how can you know if your hair is fine, medium-smooth, or thick in diameter? After all, you have nothing to compare it to. And even with the thickest hair, the diameter is so tiny that you can't take a ruler to it and measure it. However, you can determine your hair texture by paying attention to how it feels and how it falls. Take sections of hair in the front and in the back, on top and along the sides. Then look at how your hair reacts when you move it around. Does it quickly fall down flat, limp, and lifeless? Or does it stand up and puff straight out? Or does it do something in between? The more your hair falls straight down, the more it is telling you your hair is fine to medium in texture, especially if it also looks and feels lifeless and limp. Similarly, the more it likes to puff up and away from your scalp and face, the thicker the texture is likely to be. However, remember that the longer your hair is, the more likely it is to fall straight down (unless, as discussed below, your hair shape is naturally wavy or curly).

Thick hair has the widest diameter of any hair texture, noticeably wider than fine hair, and because of that it feels just a touch coarse and wiry when you run your fingers through it. It's full-bodied, dense, and strong, and masks your scalp completely (apart from any part you put in). Other good indicators: Thick hair typically takes longer to dry naturally—around an hour or more—and tends to puff up and out, away from the scalp, rather than lying flat against your head. It's this tendency to puff up and out, while also being dense and full of weight, that can make thick hair truly tough to manage, shape, and control. The right type of cut is essential. Short, heavily textured cuts that take the weight out give your hairstyle more shape and a lighter, looser look that is much easier to manage. (These heavily textured cuts don't work on midlength or long hair because all that texturizing on more than three to five inches of hair looks more like a bird's nest than a style-conscious haircut.) A long-length cut is a great alternative because long length helps weigh down thick hair so it becomes nice and straight (rather than puffing up and out as it would in a midlength cut or a shorter cut with no texture-defining layers), giving you a classic look that is easy to manage. My favorite styles for this hair type are showcased in Chapter 3, "The Ultimate Hairstyle Guide."

Fine hair feels thin and weak, light and fragile. It also lies flat against your head. No matter how much you try to fluff it up or spike it, it tends to fall back limply into place. Another way to tell: You can see through to the scalp even where the hair isn't parted. If this is you, then your hair struggles to hold its shape throughout the day, which is why cuts with soft

Thick hair

Fine hair

shape and soft lines work best for you. Strong styles with strong lines that are dependent on structure just don't hold their shape and leave you looking like a mess. You can find loads of soft-shaped haircuts, perfect for finer hair types, in Chapter 3.

Medium-smooth hair looks and feels soft and gentle and shines quite a lot. If you run your fingers through your hair and determine it's not fine, light, and limp, and not dense, thick, and coarse, then you have medium-smooth hair. You have the widest range of options—almost any style can, and will, work well for you. I've chosen a few favorites, in Chapter 3, but you can look through practically all the hair-styles in this book and decide which one is right for you.

If you're struggling to determine your texture, compare your hair with that of a few friends or relatives. You'll get a better picture of how much hair texture can vary. For example, you might touch your hair and think, "Well, it does feel a bit fine, but I'm just not sure." Maybe a friend has much thicker hair, and when you touch it, that lightbulb goes on! If you're still struggling, go into your local salon and ask for a quick consultation about your hair (there's a lot more about hair consultations on page 79). You don't have to commit to anything in a consultation—it's a free service—but you can sneak in the quick question: "So what type of hair do I have? Is it fine, medium, or thick?" Asking a professional is a sure way to get a better understanding of your hair type.

HAIR SHAPE

Your hair shape is defined by the amount of movement along the hair shaft. It falls into one of three simple categories: straight, wavy, or curly. The shape of your hair can also vary from strand to strand. It's common to have varying degrees of movement on the same head of hair, but this shouldn't pose any problems. If your hair varies from straight to wavy in shape, you can style your hair to be totally straight and smooth, or you can enhance your hair's natural movement to give you lovely flowing waves. It's all a matter of using the right styling technique. What if you're a wavy to curly hair shape? Great. There are plenty of styling techniques to help you use the uniqueness of your individual waves and curls to define your own personal style. If instead you want straightness in curly hair, using the proper styling technique makes this a fairly simple process.

To make certain you know your hair's shape, take hold of just one strand from the top of your head, near the crown. Grab it near the root and get really close to your mirror to examine its shape. Is it straight, wavy, or curly? If it's straight, it won't have any wave or wiggles, bends or curves. If it's wavy, it'll have smooth curves that go in one direction and then the other. If it's curly, it'll have a bent, twisted, or spiral shape. Now repeat this process looking at a few strands in the front, on the sides, and toward the back of your head; your hair shape can vary slightly, and in the odd case quite a lot, across the different sections of your hair. This is good to know because, for example, a lot of

Framing Your Face

Your number one priority is getting a haircut that matches the texture and shape of your hair. Then, and only then, can you think about getting a hairstyle that complements the beautiful features of your face. Most important in this respect is drawing attention toward your eyes. It may be a cliché, but it's also true: Your eyes are the windows to the soul, the focal point of your face, and your hairstyle should provide a beautiful face-framing shape. My message to you: Find a style to expose and highlight your eyes. That's where you communicate with people and it's where you have the most shape—the eyes, the cheekbones, the temples. Use this book to learn how to enhance these sensational features with Great Hair.

women have a bit more wave and movement below the crown, toward the back of the hair, than they do in the front. If you have that extra bit of movement, you can play with that wave when you're styling to give yourself more options. I'll talk a *lot* more about styling in Chapter 5, "Styling at Home."

CURLY HEADS

As you now know, it's normally the texture of your hair that is the key to finding a gorgeous low-maintenance hairstyle. Knowing your shape is generally your guide to understanding your hair better and, consequently, being able to style it better. However, if you're a true curly hair shape—you have truly spiral-shaped hair—a cut

that matches the unique natural shape of your curls makes all your styling supereasy to do. (Pages 60 to 68 describe hair styles perfect for curly hair.)

Daily Hair Care

I hear many people obsess about shampooing their hair every day. They get freaked out because they think anything less frequent results in dirty, smelly hair that doesn't look nice and clean. While I encourage everyone to have hygienically clean hair, shampooing three or four times weekly is plenty—shampoo every day only if you love that clean, fresh scent of just cleansed hair. If you do shampoo every day, use a lightweight shampoo formulated for daily use and rinse well to avoid buildup and residue. These result from the shampoo suds that are left on the scalp and eventually begin to dry it out, causing flakiness, which is often mistakenly self-diagnosed as dandruff. Hair washed every day with shampoo tends to need more styling product because it's so soft, loose, and floppy, and therefore harder to style. On the other hand, one to three days of unwashed hair result in the release of natural sebum oils from your scalp (unwashed hair means hair that has not been shampooed; you can rinse your hair with plain old water, which does not contribute to residue or affect the release of natural sebum oils). Too much of those oils can leave your hair feeling greasy, but the right amount can leave your hair with a nice easy-to-manage texture for you to

play with. If you're comfortable with natural oils, try this and see how it works for you. Just be sure to brush or quickly blow out your unwashed hair in the morning to distribute the oils and to shape and define your style. Don't use too much product, because it increases the dirt. Instead, see how you can create individual style with your own lived-in natural texture.

A final note: Some hair types—typically those with fine texture—do tend to pick up dirt and grease more quickly and may look a little too dirty to go a full three days without shampooing, but you can determine how far to push this envelope by simply looking at your hair in the mirror and making a decision to shampoo or not, based on your own preferences.

The Proper Technique for Shampooing and Conditioning Your Hair

The technique for shampooing is the same for all hair types, although the type of shampoo you use varies depending on your hair type. (See the shampoo and conditioner table on pages 14 and 15 for more help.) First, squeeze a dime-sized dab of shampoo in the palm of your hand. Then rub your palms together to create a nice lather *before* applying the shampoo to your hair. Next, spread the shampoo evenly throughout your scalp. The most common mistake is putting a big dollop of shampoo in the palms, not lathering it up, and whacking it straight onto the top of the head, then furiously trying to rub the product all over. This causes friction and damage to the cuticle (the cuticle is the outer layer of your hair shaft, the bit you can touch and see), which leads to frizz. You need to distribute the shampoo evenly. So lather up first in your palms, then apply the shampoo from below the crown and gently distribute through the rest of your hair while massaging—not rubbing—your scalp with your fingertips. In

more often than you shampoo because it's conditioner that gives you texture, moisture, and shine, all vital to lovely, luscious hair. Rinse your hair with water and then, while still in the shower or bath, apply and rinse out your conditioning product. Conditioner not only makes your hair look and feel softer and smoother, it also calms your hair down, making it easier to shape and style. For that reason it's beneficial to condition more often than you shampoo—it can be done every day if you have the time and inclination.

When applying conditioner, there's no need to overcondition the roots. Your roots are much healthier because that's where all new hair comes in. Instead of religiously trying to work conditioner through the roots, rub the product in your palms (it won't emulsify and lather like shampoo because it doesn't have the suds) and then focus your conditioning at the ends, especially when

L ight, leave-in, or daily conditioners can be left in the hair (they don't need to be rinsed out) to add a little more softness, smoothness, and shine.

addition to being the best way to clean your hair and scalp, this massage is a nice relaxing treat.

As for conditioner, there's a lot of confusion out there as to how often you need to use it. A lot of people say that you don't need to condition nearly as often as you shampoo. That's just plain wrong. I can only assume that this false notion is a result of the deeper, once-a-week conditioning treatments that are now on the market. If you're not using one of the weekly treatments, you should condition your hair

hair is more than three inches long. Focus on massaging the conditioner thoroughly through the final three inches of your hair shaft in sections all across your hair. Doing this regularly truly does make an incredible difference. Just like with shampoo, the technique is the same for all hair types, but the type of conditioner varies according to your hair. One further point: Light, leave-in, or daily conditioners can be left in the hair (they don't need to be rinsed out) to add a little more softness, smoothness, and shine—

and if the conditioner has a nice scent, that's a bonus. Make sure you rinse out thicker, more moisturizing conditioners because they weigh down the hair if they are left in.

The Proper Technique for Towel Drying Your Hair

It's best to towel-dry hair to damp (and thus ready for blow-drying and styling). But you might be surprised at how many clients come into my salon complaining of frizz and have no idea why they're stuck with this style-destroying problem. As you'll learn in Chapter 5, lots of women get frizz from using an incorrect styling technique. But this also happens when you do not towel-dry your hair properly. Many people whack the towel on their head and rub, rub, rub until it's damp, almost dry. Your hair will get dry with this method, but it's also sure to get damaged in the process.

The right way to towel-dry your hair to damp is to use your towel to gently squeeze each and every section of your hair. Move your head left and right, up and down, and gently squeeze, squeeze, squeeze until your hair is damp, not wet. Remember the last time you were at the salon, and your shampoo guy or gal gently massaged your hair with the towel after washing it? Well, that's just how you should do it every day. Rubbing your hair with a towel instead of using this squeezing technique definitely roughs

up your hair cuticles. (Remember, the cuticle is the outside portion of the hair shaft, the bit you see.) By roughing it up, you're much more likely to create frizz. With curly hair, it's better to let it dry naturally rather than use a diffuser or a blow-dryer all the time, which is what a lot of curly heads do. It's true that the more you blow-dry and diffuse genuinely curly hair, the more you can get volumized curls, but it's also true that there's a big probability of getting flyaways and frizz. Learn to style your curly hair as you let it dry naturally, allowing it to separate into a natural curl formation (see page 113 for more details on this great technique).

SHAMPOOS AND CONDITIONERS: WHICH ONE'S FOR YOU?

With so many shampoos and conditioners on the market, it can be a challenge to find the one that's right for you. Should you use daily, light, leave-in, moisturizing, or thickening products? The table on the next page explains the different features and benefits of shampoos and conditioners and what those features and benefits mean for you.

always comb from ends to roots. Start by combing through the final two to three inches of your hair—the ends of your hair shaft—and comb through to the tips. Then work your way up, combing through the next three inches or so, and continuing like this until you reach your roots. If you start at the roots and work through to the ends—the opposite direction to the correct technique just outlined—you can push all the knots in your hair together into one big tangled mess. Combing from ends to roots in easy-to-manage sections gives you your best chance to untangle any unruly knots.

The longer your hair, the more weight it has. And more weight pulls your hair down into a straight shape. In other words, if you have a slight wave or kink in your hair, the longer you wear it, the more that wave or kink falls flat, straight, and smooth. So if you want to play into the kink, go shorter; if you want a straighter, smoother look, go longer.

If you tie your long hair back almost every day, this can affect how the hair behaves. Hair tied back daily often wants to puff up and stand straight out. What do I mean? Well, when you take your hair out of a ponytail, it is naturally a bit more stand-straight-out than lie-down-nice-and-flat, but it should, after a short time, start to lie down fairly flat. If it doesn't, it's a sign that your hair has adjusted to that shape, so getting it to lie down is a challenge. If you think this is happening to you, and you're thinking about a brand-new cut, I advise you to stop tying your hair back for four to six weeks beforehand. This gives your hair time to go back into its natural shape, and it won't surprise you when you get that gorgeous new style.

If you're considering a new hairstyle, put your priorities in order. Numbers one, two, and three are the potentials of your hair. What hairstyles can your hair most naturally achieve to give you your best chance to create gorgeous, fun hair with minimal fuss? This is how I approach every single haircut for every single client. It's the key to my success, and I'm sure it'll be the key to your success, too. (There's a lot more help on shapes and styles to suit each individual in Chapters 2 and 3, so if you're getting excited about trying a new you, those are great places to start.)

I encourage you all to keep changing and adapting the way you look. Change invigorates us and makes us feel younger, more confident, sexier, healthier, more vibrant, and more modern. I certainly suggest taking a good look at your hairstyle every year and asking yourself if it's time for an inspirational new you.

No matter what your hair type, your everyday challenges, whether you have out-of-control frizzies, dry, damaged hair, wild flyaways, unmanageably thick hair, fine, fragile hair, or even an unusual combination of all the common problems, there's a 100 percent chance of achieving a look you love, especially when you start by getting the right style for your hair type.

Summing It All Up

Chapter 1 of your Great Hair journey is all about getting to know and understand your own hair type. You should now know your own hair's shape and texture and the important role that plays in finding the right hairstyle for you. If your hair has fine texture, look for a haircut and style that create volume and thickness and life in your hair. If your hair has medium-smooth texture, you now know that most hairstyles suit you perfectly well and you can begin to think about your own preferences. If your hair has thick texture, you know that you're looking for a hairstyle that creates space and freedom, and that defeats the puffiness and bulk that can cause problems for you. If your hair shape is naturally curly, you want a cut and style that celebrate your curls by playing into the strengths of your unique hair type. Whatever your type, picking a style that suits your own texture and shape gives you your best chance of getting a modern, style-defining haircut that beautifully frames the features of your face.

By now you are aware that different hair types (and different people) need different shampoos and conditioners, and choosing the right combination for you plays an important part in the overall integrity of your hair. Get this simple element right and you have a great foundation for moving forward with Great Hair.

Finally, my Golden Guidelines and my refutation of the major myths and legends surrounding hair care will help keep you on the straight-and-narrow road to successful style.

Old Wives' Tales

There are many misguided ideas about hair. Mistaken beliefs about what you should and shouldn't do have been circulating in homes and around the hair salons of the world for centuries. They may appear harmless and even quite comforting, but the misguided gospel they teach does affect your ability to create Great Hair. We definitely don't want that, so let's cut through the myths and the legends.

Hair Grows Faster If You Trim It

I'm sure this myth comes from the fact that trimming ends makes your hair look healthier. That is true because you're cutting off all those nasty split ends, but hair grows at the same rate no matter how often you cut or trim it. If you're trying to grow

your hair longer, wait a bit longer in between cuts. Wait until your hair has grown three inches and then ask your hairdresser to cut off an inch. You have two more inches than when you started growing it, and by cutting off an inch, you give your hairdresser the opportunity to cut in some shape and style. Continue this process until your hair reaches your desired length. Not only is your hair now nice and long, but its health is in tip-top shape, too.

Cutting Your Hair Short Makes It Thicker

No, it doesn't. Cutting hair short gives the *illusion* of thickness. When hair is on the longer side, the extra weight pulls it down, making it look fine and thin. Conversely, short hairs lie on top of each other and with that comes the illusion of thicker hair. If you have fine or thinning hair, a shorter style might be just the ticket.

Product Doesn't Make a Difference

Unless you have a crew cut or a shaved head, product does make a great difference in styling. Without product, clean hair is definitely less easy to style. But you don't need a hatful of products to make your hair work. Of course, you can have fun trying lots of products and experimenting with what works best for your hair, but you really need only a small selection of products that work well for you.

Think about your styling products in two categories. Category one consists of some foundation-building products, and category two features one or two products that give a fabulous finish to your look. Your foundation product—for example, volumizing foam, styling crème, texturizing paste, or hair crèmes or lotions—creates shape and structure; finishing products like shine spray, holding spray, or hair spray add the final dazzling touches and/or hold your look in place. First and foremost, use products that work for you, but I also advise trying to find complementary products from the same product line. Good-quality styling lines are designed to work together and the fragrances will be complementary, too. (There's more on choosing the right styling products for you on page 92.)

Color Treatments Thicken Your Hair

A chemical color treatment won't thicken your hair, but it may alter the texture slightly. When color is deposited, it can—especially if it's a radical color change like bleaching—expand your hair shaft temporarily, adding an extra dimension of fullness that gives you thicker texture, more volume, and more grip (what I mean is that the hair "grips" onto pins more easily—great for when you're pinning your hair back or into an updo). Play into this illusion of thickness by putting a bit more hold and volume into your blow-dry. But color *only* if you want new color, not for thickness, because only the color can be guaranteed; the added texture can't. If you find a bit of added texture after coloring, it's a bonus, and make as much out of it as you can! Remember, color adds depth and richness to the texture because it reflects light in a more flattering way, again giving the illusion your hair is full and thick.

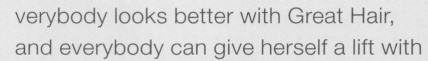

2. The Power of the Makeover

Everybody looks better with Great Hair, and everybody can give herself a lift with a great change to the way she looks. I truly believe that if you look great, you feel fabulous. But so many people are afraid or unwilling to make that change. Some become attached to a certain hairstyle or to wearing their hair long; they make it part of who they are, and they're never going to change that. Well, I'm all for making hair part of who you are, but not if it's making you look dated, old-fashioned, and dull. As the years fly by, all of our personalities change and adapt. So should your hair. It should be part of your personality in a much better way than being known as the woman who kept her hair the same for sixty years, like Queen Elizabeth. If this is true for you, be honest with yourself. Take a long, hard look in the mirror and ask: "Does my hair look healthy and sexy? Does it improve upon my natural beauty?" If not, it's time for a change.

If you're a working woman, your hair should make you look polished and professional; if you're a busy mom, it should make you look stylish and pulled together; if you're young and hip, it should make you look young and hip; if you're older and want to disguise your age, your hair should make you look younger, fresher, more modern. Hair is the best and easiest way to convey a look or create a positive impression. It's

not like cosmetic surgery, where going under the knife is a considerable risk. If you cut your hair too short for you, it grows back! If you don't like the style, get another one. If the color is not for you, it's so easy to change. See what I'm saying? Make hair an accessory to who you are and don't be afraid to change it as you go. Maybe in your twenties you are a rocker chick. Fantastic. Get a rocker chick hairstyle (Kelly wears a great one on page 60). By the time you reach thirty, you may be a professional working for a record company, and that's the time to make your hair more professional, too. Later you may want a cut that helps you look more youthful. You can do that as well—by changing your hairstyle.

Here are before-and-after shots of some women who were in real need of a powerful makeover. These women had become complacent about their frazzled and frumpy hairstyles. In each case her hair made her look older and less pretty. That was a terrible shame, because these women are *beautiful.* They just needed to be brave and get a haircut that comes close to matching their own inner and outer beauty. Thankfully, they plucked up the courage. Believe me, there were many tears of sadness as I cut off those long locks, but you know what? As soon as they saw their brand-new style, their brand-new selves, tears of joy began to flow. They told me they felt different and better than they'd felt in years. They were certainly ready for a night on the town! These women found the courage to make a change. I hope they inspire the same from you.

When I first saw Stefanie, her hair looked

lank and limp and shapeless. Her youthful features made her a great candidate for a new look.

When I looked closely at Stefanie's hair, I noticed some beautiful natural wave and curl movements. I wanted to give her options for curly and straight styling. This is a classic bob length with graduated layers—perfect to style straight and perfect to style curly. She looks sensational.

Stefanie's straight look shows how versatile her haircut is. I used a blow-dryer and then a straightening iron to create this sleek, movable, and sexy straight style. She looks professional and pulled together.

Rachel came to me with long, beautiful, healthy hair,

but she needed a style and was ready for magic. We donated her cutoff hair to Locks of Love, a very worthy cause,[*] and because she was willing to lose all that length, it gave me a fantastic opportunity for invention.

The finished style is a versatile and soft, choppy, graduated razor-cut bob. It's playful and sexy, and it elegantly exposes Rachel's neck to give height to her petite frame.

*Locks of Love is a nonprofit organization that provides wigs for financially disadvantaged children who have lost their hair due to illness. http://locksoflove.org.

Nicole had never had a style before, and her superlong,

way-past-the-waist, heavy hair had no shape or style. Her petite but full figure gets no benefits from this mane. Another lovely head of hair donated to Locks of Love, allowing the girl to look truly beautiful in the process.

I cut this style to just above the shoulder for maximum lift and softness. It's layered throughout to uncover her gorgeous natural hair for a simple wash-and-wear style, every day.

Ashlee had lots of lank hair. The high, exposed forehead

with fluffy, expanded sides to the collarbone created no shape or definition for her beautiful face. This made Ashlee look heavier than she really is, because we couldn't see her cheekbones.

This is a fun, short razor cut with long bangs to soften the forehead and create emphasis on the top, which gives lift to the whole face. This is a playful, youthful, and pretty easy-to-wear style. Ashlee now has emphasis at the eyes and cheekbones, which gives more shine to her appearance.

Adrian had thick, long, and heavy unstyled hair.

It had no shape whatsoever with a strong cowlick hair growth line at the front.

A classic collarbone-length razor cut gives instant shape and swing. The long layers allow for versatility, and I used a curling iron for her second style option: It's a softer, more carefree look that is both playful and sexy.

Mariana was just fifteen when we met her.

She is naturally beautiful, but her long heavy hair over-powered her look.

What a fantastic difference this classic long layer cut made. I removed the heaviness of the hair to free up the swing, while the soft, dimensional color adds prettiness. Now she has a lots of different styling options.

Sara is another woman whose long, heavy hair was

weighing her down. I gave her freshness with a more
youthful and contemporary look.

This is a lovely soft layer style cut to the collarbone.
As you can see from the two images, Sara can now
blow her hair out for a sleeker but swinging look,
or she can leave in her natural wave in a carefree,
modern style.

3. The Ultimate Hairstyle Guide

N ow that you know your hair and you've seen the power of the makeover, you should be ready to make a style-defining change for yourself. To help you on that journey, this Ultimate Hairstyle Guide displays twenty-eight different haircuts divided into categories that show you the best kinds of cuts for fine, medium-smooth, and thick hair types, with a separate section for curly hair.

I'm not fond of hard-and-fast rules, so if you see a style that's not in your category but think it could be good for you, that's great. Show it to your stylist and get his or her opinion on how it might work for you and your hair texture. Ask for some styling techniques that will make it easy to manage from day to day. If your stylist thinks that particular hairstyle is too much of a stretch for your hair type, ask if there is a similar style that is a better fit. I do believe that if you have truly fine, thick, or curly hair, the haircuts in that category will be your best fit. For medium-smooth hair types, the cuts displayed for you are some of my favorite options, but your hair generally suits most hairstyles—you can pick and choose from any of the categories.

All these wonderful women are real people—not a professional model in sight. That's because I wanted to show you how these real haircuts

33

work for real women. Remember, if you use hair as an accessory, getting the right kind of look and being polished and youthful is easy.

Each cut is a modern classic and will keep you looking fresh and contemporary for many years to come. Some require a little more day-to-day work than others, but I made sure that they are all pretty easy to manage. With any of these styles there's a twenty-minute morning commitment that will have you looking sensational, and when you have the time or occasion to do more, use my tips in Chapters 5 and 9 to spruce yourself up even more. First, though, use this guide for inspiration and ideas. I'm sure you'll find a hairstyle that is the perfect fit for you right here, right now, as well as some alternative styles that will be your perfect fit a year—or two—from now.

I have included a few more short styles than longer ones. For long hair, there are two basic options: layer your long hair or go for a one-length haircut. Both are great ways to wear your hair and you can certainly change it up a bit by going for bangs or not, and of course ponytails and twists are another great way to wear your hair. But if the hair is shorter, then for the actual style there are multiple ways to go. Bobs (rounded, graduated, and straight), shags, messy short layer cuts, pixie cuts, and more all become completely achievable. By considering a few more shorter styles than longer ones, you get the widest range of options.

Along with images, I've added descriptions of how and why the cuts work so well, along with quick and easy styling ideas suited to each individual cut. I expand on these ideas in Chapter 5, but this is a great quick-reference guide if you get so excited about your new do that you want to get styling started right away.

Finally, don't be afraid to take this book to your hairdresser and say, "I want this style." It's the ideal way to show your stylist exactly what you want to achieve. Cutting, styling, and photographing this chapter were a true labor of love. I hope you enjoy wearing the hair as much as I enjoyed creating it!

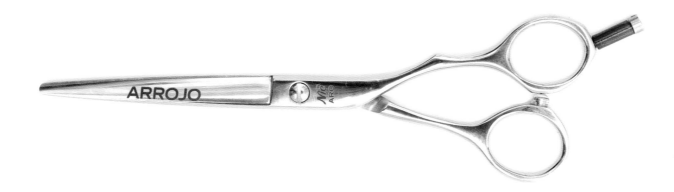

Great Cuts for Fine Hair

KENDALL

The Style. This is an archetypal mid-length to long heavily layered cut, hugely popular because it's so feminine and easy to wear. Although Kendall's hair is superdense, it is also fine and wispy, and these heavy layers really help to create the illusion of thickness. Kendall's hair also has a beautiful natural wave, and I played into this by giving her strong, side-swept bangs that have shape and movement, and that accentuate her strong cheekbones and pretty eyes. The subtle combination highlighting looks sensational. I used different tones of dark blond highlights running all through her hair for a polished, sophisticated, stand-out style.

Stylability. I gave Kendall a smooth blow out with a medium-sized round brush, first applying a volume enhancer and a serum. The volume product is almost essential if the hair is fine and being worn relatively long—otherwise it can look a bit thin and flat. It's far better to lift and thicken up your hair with a good bodybuilder. The serum just helps to keep the smooth blow-dry ultrasmooth. Once I was finished with that, all that was needed was to use the fingers to tousle out the roots, playing into the looseness and freedom of the cut. That's all quick and easy to do and should take you no more than fifteen minutes. Want to change it? Easy. You can pull the hair back and pin it into any kind of bun,

twist, or ponytail. All will look great, especially if your hair has a natural wave to it. If it doesn't, use your round brush and blow-dryer to create some! Then just use a holding spray to make sure your pinned-back do stays fixed into place.

LARISSA

The Style. Larissa's hair is borderline fine to medium with a gorgeous natural shine. This modern, jaw-length bob with soft and gentle layers promotes the illusion of extra thickness and volume while the clean lines and soft shape show off the health of her hair. The side-swept bangs showcase simple, classic style and they elongate her features. The bangs also bring attention to her bright, sparkly eyes. For the color, all I wanted to do was play into her shimmering, shiny hair, and this dark chocolate tone with tints of red adds texture, thickness, shine, and dimension.

Stylability. As Larissa's hair is a touch fine and superstraight, I used a volume-enhancing product, applied from roots to ends of damp hair, and followed that with a round brush blow-dry. This quickly and easily creates an extra kick of body and bounce, while retaining the sense of loose freedom and movement in the style. This freedom and movement is a modern look, but if you want to set the style with more hold and structure, a blow-dry setting spray, lotion, or crème, again complemented with a round brush blow-dry, gives you more firmness and hold. Styling this soft, gently layered bob is achievable inside fifteen minutes, ten with practice.

MARY

The Style. Mary's short and choppy shag has textured layers all through the front, top, sides, and back. The beauty of this is that it promotes a soft, cascading, carefree sort of style. Though it looks (and is) loose and natural, the actual haircut requires the stylist to create a lot of structure in the shape. The right structure gives lift and volume through the top of the haircut, which adds bounce and spring—and that creates extra youthfulness, making this a great style for ladies who would like their hair to help them look younger and more vibrant. Mary has natural light brown hair, and I used subtle high- and lowlighting all around her bangs, which gives an extra illusion of lift, softens her complexion, and draws attention to her eyes.

Stylability. Styling this kind of haircut is easy. The aim is to create extra volume at the roots and a soft and tousled effect toward the ends. Not too much volume, though, just enough to give it some movement. I used a light, easy-to-apply volume foam at the roots and blow-dried Mary's hair using a small round brush to get right in toward her roots, lifting them up and away from her scalp. Then I used a hair crème at the ends to give a bit more sheen and polish. It all took ten to fifteen minutes, tops. If you go for a style like this and want a change to your look, you can use a texturizing paste and play into the choppy layers and pieciness even more. Apply from roots to ends and focus on creating separation in the style. Do this and you could forgo the blow-dry completely.

ALLY

The Style. This is one of my favorite shaggy, featherweight styles, and it is a perfect cut for Ally. Her relatively fine hair also has a natural wave to it, which plays into the shape of the cut, and she doesn't need to worry about such a loose, free style holding its shape, which is always a challenge for fine hair. Technically speaking, this may be termed a square layer cut, but all I really did was use the razor to free up the hair into a loose and modern, easy-to-wear style. You can see how the length drapes effortlessly around Ally's cheeks, and this helps to slim down and frame the features of the face. Once again, the color is simply an enrichment of her natural shade. In this case a medium brown single process with tiny tints of red for an extra touch of glisten and shine.

Stylability. I like to describe this style as wash-and-wear. Even if Ally jumped out of the shower and did absolutely nothing to her hair, I'd still put my razor on the line and say it would look fabulous. In this case, though, I used a curl-enhancing product and a setting crème. Although her hair clearly is not curly, the curl product just gives sexy wave and movement in the hair while the setting crème adds a touch of volume, since the hair is on the fine side. Other than that, I just finger-styled the look until we were happy with the shape—that's easily achievable for anyone.

MOLLY

The Style. Molly has baby-fine hair, so it was important to give her a look that offers that vital illusion of fullness. This long layer cut with the layers sweeping in toward the face does just that. The layers begin at the jawline for face-framing shape and continue long past her shoulders for a nice, soft finish. The wide, curved, and full bangs also enhance the illusion of thickness, as well as draw attention to her eyes. A perfect, polished do that is great for a style-conscious woman of any age. For the color, Molly came to us with tired-looking bleached blond hair with the roots of her natural brown showing through. I introduced heavy highlighting that adds gloss and sheen, making Molly a truly beautiful blonde.

Stylability. With the previous bleaching process and the need for strong highlighting, Molly's hair is prone to frizz and flyaways. So the key in the styling is to calm any potential frizz and also give her fine hair an extra kick of volume. I applied a volume foam from roots to ends and a defrizz product from the midlengths through to the ends. I blow-dried it smooth with a round brush and high heat, before finishing off the look with a straightening iron to help smooth out the ends even more. This is a classy cut that you can style quickly and easily each morning.

PEGGY

The Style. Peggy's hair is fine and also a bit fragile, so she needed a cut that would add structure and volume. The perfect solution is this shoulder-length, light face-frame cut with multiple layering. The layers begin around the cheekbones to frame the face, and the longer length in the back keeps it feminine. The cut is designed to be soft, loose, and easy to wear. All-over blond highlights increase the blond bombshell factor and get those great blue eyes popping perfectly. A great cut for anyone worried that her fine hair is destroying her style.

Stylability. For such fine hair, volume foam is the go-to product, and I applied it from roots to ends as a volume-building base that lifts, thickens, and supports the style. I also applied a moisture-giving hair crème to help smooth out and polish the look. After that you can blow-dry straight with a round brush or a flat paddle brush, or you can use a curling iron to add an extra dose of wave and movement. Both ways are showcased here and are achievable inside fifteen minutes. It's easy and sure to make you feel like a million dollars. As a plus, the length makes simple ponytails and twists great styling options.

ALEX

The Style. Wow! What wonderful natural silver-gray hair. Alex's hair is rather fine and light, but this superstrong one-length line and dramatic bangs creates the perfect shape for her. Her gray hair is truly beautiful, and that's what I wanted to play into with this one-length haircut. It also exposes her cheekbones, elongating her facial features (for extra youthfulness) in the process. The vivid, striking bangs portray a powerful, polished woman and a marvelous, modern finish. The natural color is so charismatic that it needed no color enhancement at all—it shows you don't always need to hide or mask gray.

Stylability. Gray hair can be frizzy, and to style such an easy one-length cut, all I had to think about was making sure all that gray hair looked supersmooth. To do this, I blow-dried with a flat paddle brush, using only a touch of defrizz serum and a dab of hair crème. The serum eliminates the frizz while the hair crème smoothes out and polishes the look. This look is totally achievable inside fifteen minutes for anyone. And with such sensational bangs, a sophisticated low or dramatic high ponytail would looks fab.

Great Cuts for Medium-Smooth Hair

BOONSRI

The Style. This is an ultramodern, long, layered bob, cut to the collarbone. The razor cutting adds texture and playful pieciness right through to the ends. The shape of the cut brings definition to the cheeks; the full, straight, and square bangs beautifully frame her face; and the structure makes this a real head turner. A darkish brown single-process hair color is accented with ribbons of soft highlights. The highlights give an extra touch of dimension to the cut but are subtle and fine enough to look polished and sophisticated. A modern cut and color for a modern woman, and just look at how the full bangs, accented with highlights, make Boonsri's beautiful blue eyes explode.

Stylability. Another easy-to-achieve do. I applied a volume-building styling crème to set her look and a frizz-fighting serum as just an extra source of smoothness. I blow-dried the hair with a flat paddle brush, focusing on making it smooth and straight. If you go for a similar style, you can do the same. The blow-dry should take no more than fifteen minutes, but if that's too long for you, you can easily substitute a straightening iron for your brush and blow-dryer. Work it quickly and easily through the top, sides, front, and back, and you'll be golden.

CAITLIN

The Style. Caitlin wears a short, graduated razor cut with lots of length at the top to create a wispy and light short-to-long feel. This gives the short shape pieciness and movement with soft edges, and a side part sweeps across the face, drawing attention to her eyes. It's a fun and flirty hairstyle. Caitlin had some previous uneven color, so this demipermanent brown touch evens out her hair color while adding shine and definition.

Stylability. Short styles are easy to manage, control, and manipulate. I used only a tiny amount of product to keep the style soft and movable. To get this look, mix a dab of texture paste and a dab of hair crème in your palm, and use your fingers to texturize the cut, keeping it relatively loose and messy, with a sexy matte finish. Or use the versatility of the cut to have fun shaping all sorts of different styles. Move the part to the left or to the right; mess it up or smooth it out; even use a bit more product to spike it up into a more vampish style. You need only ten minutes to make yourself look cool and contemporary, not to mention sexy and sophisticated.

BRIGHTON

The Style. This is a youthful, choppy bob with bangs. The back is razor-cut quite short, up to the nape of her neck, and this helps to build structure and allows the hair to become elevated, which gives the impression of volume you see here. I also used the razor to put in some random layers, giving the hair separation and pieciness. As you can see, there's no definite line in the bangs; they've just been texturized to be movable, carefree, and easy. This is a great cut for a hip young girl—it's a modern, edgy, and fun way to wear the hair. For the color, I just used subtle highlighting for depth and dimension.

Stylability. There's so much looseness and freedom in the cut that the styling is ever so easy. I used a texture paste on wet hair and blow-dried it using my fingers to shape the style. You can do the same inside ten or fifteen minutes. Change it by moving the placement of the part or messing it up even more for an oh-so-sexy, just-rolled-out-of-bed look.

NADIA

The Style. This classic short and layered graduation is perfect for Nadia's classically medium-smooth hair texture. Again, her hair has been razor-cut quite short at the back, right up to the nape—a great technique to lift the shape and add fullness and volume. The bangs sweep elegantly across her face; they create softness and a little sassiness for Nadia's newly polished do. Again, the emphasis is on a light and loose, modern, easy-to-wear haircut that promotes youthfulness and beauty in a client-friendly I-can-shape-this-style sort of way. This cut is one of my first choices for a client, perhaps in her forties, fifties, or sixties, who wants to look younger. The short, soft shape helps a lot. For the color, an allover chestnut demipermanent single-process accented with subtle high- and lowlighting in the bangs softens the complexion and adds dimension to the shape of the cut.

Stylability. The shape of this cut makes styling easy. It wants to be loose and messy, and that's your focus in shaping it at home. I used a texture paste and a styling crème mixed together in my palms and then worked it through the top, sides, middle, and back, from roots to ends of damp hair. Following that came a quick blast of heat from the dryer, with only the fingers to style the hair as you see it here—supple and free. That's all you need to do, too. To add a bit more glamour and glitz, a shine or holding spray polishes up the finish even more.

CHRIS

The Style. Lucky Chris! Her hair is smooth, shiny, and straight, which gives her a lot of great options. I went for this signature box bob with bangs. The hair was scissor-cut to make sure the lines were clean and symmetrical, which enhances the healthy appearance of her hair. The full, straight bangs create the width that opens up her eyes for an ultramodern and youthful look. The color is an espresso bean single process, an enhancement of her natural color that really brings out the sultry shine. A style-savvy do that is brilliant for youthfulness and natural beauty.

Stylability. The key in styling such a straight and smooth look is to enhance these elements. I applied a defrizz serum from the midlengths to the ends and blow-dried on a high heat with a flat brush. Though Chris's hair is not particularly prone to frizz, serum also straightens and smooths out all hair types, and that's exactly what it's done here. This look of a bold and confident woman can be achieved with a fifteen-minute blow-dry.

LAUREEN

The Style. Laureen has beautiful, shiny, medium-smooth hair. I layered her long one-length cut into this slightly shorter, more polished look. The bangs are side parted and sweep elegantly across her bright, flickering eyes. This graceful, cultured, and sophisticated style adds youthfulness and beauty in an easy-to-wear way. The color is a dark brown enhancement of her natural hue and fits well with Laureen's complexion.

Stylability. The shape of the cut makes this so easy to style. If you want to keep it straight and smooth, apply a volume foam from roots to ends with a styling or setting crème or lotion, also from roots to ends. Together the products build structure and hold the look in place. After the product application, blow-dry with a round or flat brush in smooth, straight, and easy motions. This takes around twenty minutes, but you can quicken it up by using a straightening iron instead. To create some sexy flowing waves for a night out, or even just for a change, use a curling iron to wave and twist the hair, resulting in a more flirty approach, as I did with Laureen's more curly style.

LEE

The Style. Lee wears this short, choppy, and oh-so-cute pixie cut. A great style for the young and trendy, and anyone who wants a great hairdo with a minimum of fuss in the styling. I razor-cut it into this playful, messy texture with a few longer, wispy bits left in the back for a touch more femininity. The short style brings out all the features in Lee's face while the broken-up bangs filter beautifully into the eyes. For the color, a face-framing highlight adds a touch of sparkle and embellishes the fun, flirty nature of the cut.

Stylability. It doesn't get any easier than this! Even leaving the hair unshampooed for a few days gives awesome natural texture, meaning there's no need to blow-dry at all. Don't worry, hair this short doesn't get too greasy. If that's not for you, then do what I did and apply a texture-giving paste, gel, or crème. Just have fun working it in and see what kind of textures you can create. You can slick it straight for a smooth matte finish, or mess it up for a punchy slept-in look.

Great Cuts for Thick Hair

JESSICA

The Style. Jessica has such sweet, warm, and doll-like facial features that the idea was to bring out this beauty in the cut. Her hair is thick, so this classic short and textured cropped razor cut makes her hair ultramanageable and ultraversatile. Short, textured waves and layers are a great option when you want to add strength and definition to the face, and they make thick hair easy to manage, but in a soft and loose way. It's a free and messy style with a rich, dark brown single-process color tone, accented with hints of red. The matte finish of this color enhances the shape of the cut and provides the perfect contrast to her skin tone.

Stylability. Even though longer hair can be pulled up or down into all sorts of ponytails and twists, short hair is the most versatile for styling. You can finger-style it into a messy shape, spike it up, smooth it out, and even blow it dry with a round or vent brush, or use your fingers to create a little more wave and movement. In this instance, I used a texturizing paste for the separation you see here along with a moisture-rich hair crème to polish up the look. Mix the two together and apply from roots to ends on damp hair, before giving it a superquick blast of heat from the blow-dryer, aided by some gentle finger styling to create a soft, textured, and lightly messy look, just as Jessica wears it here. For hair

this short, texturizing paste and a light-hold hair crème are your two go-to products, although a volume-building styling or setting crème gives the look extra lift, and a shine spray adds dazzle for the finish. A totally quick and easy hairstyle giving you control and flexibility—five minutes in the morning is all you need.

HILARY

The Style. This is one of my signature styles. I love a classic graduated razor bob cut with a soft symmetrical line. It's a great option for thick hair because the cut creates looseness, swing, and movement for hair that is normally weighed down. It's cut to just below the jaw, making a perfect frame for her face, while the bangs are also razor cut, making them a touch choppy, as they drape effortlessly just above the eyes. Here is a truly modern way to wear your hair. Hilary has naturally red hair, a beautiful rarity that I left as it was.

Stylability. For this sort of style, you want to create smoothness as well as volume. A quick blow out with volume-enhancing product and a flat brush is your ticket to get the style quickly and easily, in ten or fifteen minutes. I applied a volume foam to dampened hair and blow-dried, using the wraparound technique (illustrated on page 102). This added extra smoothness to the look. To change it, you can adjust the placement of your part or try the volumizing blow-out (page 107). A great way to add extra body and bounce to any kind of hairstyle.

MELISSA

The Style. Melissa has lovely thick, strong hair, making her a great candidate for this sharp, bold look. The razor cut with sweeping bangs brings out the power in her eyes. It's also heavily layered all through the top, which creates a lot of freedom for Melissa to wear her hair messy or smooth, spiked or flat. This is a fun hairstyle and great if you want a hip hairstyle that requires little or no maintenance. The color is a half-blue, half-black single process that is dark and ultrashiny, a great contrast to her crystal clear eyes.

Stylability. There's lots of versatility here, and even if you do nothing at all it still looks great. In this instance, I just used a blow-dryer, finger styling, and a shine spray. Shine spray not only shines up short hair, it also fights flyaways, keeping the hair flat and smooth. Ten minutes and the style is yours. And you can easily change the part placement. Add a dime-sized dab of texture paste, applied from roots to ends, and you can make a much messier, more rock-and-roll style as well. A great all-rounder that offers the modern woman lots of options.

ANNE

The Style. Anne wears a creative, graphic shape with heavy emphasis on the bangs. The strong outline frames the features of her face, but by using the razor, I kept the back loose and shaggy, which gives Anne the choice of smooth or messy. (You can see the difference in the photos.) Her thick, straight hair now swings and moves with flexibility and freedom. It's a bold and edgy cut that is fun and easy to wear. For the color, I used a single-process dark chocolate to add extra shine and definition to her already lusty hair.

Stylability. The versatility of this cut makes it great for styling at home. To keep it smooth, apply a smoothing crème or lotion from roots to ends and blow-dry with a flat or round brush with the aim of keeping it smooth and straight. Added shine brings out the definition of the cut, so I finished with a light film of shine spray spread evenly across the hair, which is great for visible gloss and an elegant, polished finish. Or for the messy, slept-in look, simply work a texture-giving paste, gel, or crème from roots to ends of damp hair and make a messy style your focus—a supercool way to wear this style and a great look for a night on the town. If you're planning to work by day and play by night, you can even stick the texturizer in your bag and work it in after office hours to create that striking change, perfect for parties.

to give Stephanie's hair the movement and softness she craved, while still keeping the length long. This opened up and slimmed down her facial features. And, as you see, I gave her long and sexy sweeping bangs that cut across her eyes beautifully. This means that Stephanie can now style her hair straight when she wants to look polished and professional, and she can style her hair into sultry waves when she wants to look extrahot. For the color, soft highlights were the order of the day. Lighter than her natural color, these give the illusion of a lighter hair texture and sit effortlessly all around her face, bringing out her great complexion.

Stylability. Two contrasting but equally fabulous looks make this a standout style. Stephanie can use a smoothing lotion or even a defrizz serum with a blow-dryer and flat brush to blow-dry the hair smooth and straight for an elegant and refined style. Or, to bring the sexy back, she can ramp it up by using the natural wave in her hair to create flowing, tousled locks that are a real head turner. To do that, she blow-dries her hair loosely, without a brush, until it is around 80 percent dry. Then all she has to do is apply hair crème or styling crème together with a shine spray, from roots to ends. Then she can just cup and scrunch her hair to her heart's content. Cupping and scrunching really works in the wave—deliciously attractive. As her hair is long and thick, the smooth blow out takes around twenty minutes, but for such a sophisticated style it's worth the effort. The second style needs to be scrunched periodically until the hair is dry.

STEPHANIE

The Style. Stephanie's hair is thick, long, and luscious with a nice natural wave. That's great, but prior to this cut she was being weighed down by all the density and her cut had no true shape. I started by scissor-cutting away the extra weight and cutting in long and loose layers

LAURA

The Style. Laura's hair is long and superthick. Before she came to us it was also full of excessive volume, a typical problem with thick hair. To cut that out, and get more freedom and movement in the style, I went for this long layer cut, which makes the hair soft and bouncy looking. I didn't cut in any bangs; her long, thick hair off the face exposes her wonderful, bubbly features. Her hair is a lovely natural brown, which suits her so well that color was not needed.

Stylability. To get this voluptuous look, I set Laura's hair in loose rollers. I used volume foam from the roots to the ends to build some structure, and a setting lotion, mainly focused at the roots, before clipping her into rollers for thirty minutes, releasing, and then finishing the style with a brush, blow-dry, and a mist of holding spray. That's too much work for every morning, but it's great for any sort of occasion, especially a date—the result is supersexy and likely to drive your man crazy! For a more user-friendly day-to-day do, simply blow-dry the hair with a round brush and use a volume foam or a styling lotion or crème to build up the style.

MORGAN

The Style. Morgan has thick hair and I wanted to maximize the appearance of volume and fullness. This collar-length layer cut, swept off the face, does just that. It looks soft and carefree, yet with structure and strength. A modern style perfect for shapely looks and versatility. The face-framing, multidimensional highlight is lighter than her natural color and also gives the illusion of volume.

Stylability. This one is easy to style straight and easy to style wavy. For the straight look, I used volume foam, applied at the roots and worked through to the ends, as another source of fullness, before blow-drying her hair in a straight line with a round brush, finishing the look with a holding spray, another great tool to help hair hold its shape. Putting in wave and movement is easy, too. The easiest way is to use a curling iron to create tousled loose waves around the face, the sides, and the back, anywhere you crave it. If you fancy it, you can even pin the hair into place after you've put the waves in. Pinning in your waves with bobby pins holds them in place, ensuring your waves look sexy and sophisticated all day, all night. And they're perfect for any occasion. The shape of this cut makes styling a breeze, and fifteen or twenty minutes should be enough to get you looking fashionably elegant.

Great Cuts for Curly Hair

KELLY

The Style. Kelly's medium-smooth, curly hair is a great fit for this full-bodied, curl-enhancing cut. It's a scissor cut and has been heavily layered throughout to create the space and freedom that accentuate the shapeliness and allow for modern movement in curly hair. I deliberately cut the bangs short to expose her forehead, creating a slim-line effect. The blond highlights really make Kelly's striking blue eyes pop with feminine beauty. This provides a nice balancing effect because this loose, wearable cut was inspired by Kelly's love of rock music and is definitely in the rock star–style category.

Stylability. Oh so easy. After the cut, all I did to style this fabulous look was apply a touch of curl-enhancing product and a touch of moisture-giving hair crème, one after the other, from roots to ends, on damp hair. The curl enhancer defines the shape of the curls while the hair crème softens, smoothes, and keeps any potential frizz at bay. I let the hair dry naturally, and then, to hold the style in place, used a midhold hairspray, which sets the style for the whole day. (This isn't essential, so if you're in a rush and want to leave the house while your hair continues to air dry, no problem.) If you feel like ramping up the styling a notch, apply your first two products as outlined, but dry your hair with a diffuser rather then letting it air-

dry. A diffuser is easy to use and would give this style an extra kick of fullness and volume, great for a night on the town. A diffuser can induce frizz, so apply a more liberal amount of hair crème and don't overdry. Then wait for the admiring glances you'll get for such bouncy, voluptuous, curly hair.

AUBRIE

The Style. Aubrie has lovely natural curls that are vibrant and full of character and volume. Her only trouble is that there are lots of them and her hair is thick, too, which makes tangled-together curls a real possibility—and a real style destroyer. To prevent this, and to let Aubrie wear those natural curls naturally, I created a heavily layered rounded cut with a strong structure that holds the shape of her curls. The strong structure allows the curls to stack on top of each other, while the point-cutting technique (cutting the hair from a vertical angle instead of the more traditional horizontal angle) offers enough space so that we can see the beautiful texture in her hair. A truly natural curl-enhancing cut. For the color, I used a midlevel brown glaze at the roots, which matches Aubrie's natural hair color, but a touch of added color brings out that brown in a nice and shiny way. There are a few highlights, too, because this is a great way to showcase the definition in the curls.

Stylability. I believe that the best way to style curly hair is with a cut that celebrates the curls and gives them enough space to move. Then styling curly hair, considered a nightmare by many curly heads, is totally free and easy. All I did for Aubrie was give her a cut that plays into her natural curly hair texture. And what did I do to style it? Barely anything at all. Into damp hair I put a curl-enhancing crème to bring out the shape of her curls and a styling crème just to hold and set the look in place. No blow-drying; I simply cupped and squeezed her hair all over

for two minutes at a time, every fifteen minutes or so, until it was dry. And that's it, easy as pie. It may take awhile for the hair to dry naturally, but you don't have to wait around the house while this is happening, Apply the product, leave the house if you need to, and just remember to cup and squeeze every fifteen minutes until dry. (Want to know more about this technique? Check out Chapter 5, "Styling at Home," and "Controlled Curls," page 113.)

HEIDI

The Style. Heidi has naturally fine and moderately curly hair, which can be a bit of a problem if you don't get the right kind of cut. The shape and definition of the curls are likely to fall flat, and often you're left wondering whether to style your hair straight or curly. I went for a classic short and round, heavily layered do. This provides structure and shape for her lovely, luscious hair that celebrates her curl formation, while also giving the option of an easy, straight style. The cut creates elevation for her features and brings emphasis back where it belongs: the eyes. The color is a rich red and auburn single process that suits her complexion and looks shiny, glossy, and burnished.

Stylability. To enhance the soft, natural curl in Heidi's hair, I used a curl-enhancing product and simply twisted the curls around my index finger to get that gorgeous spiral shape and exquisite round structure for the style. If that sounds like too much work for you, use the same product but replace your fingers with a curling iron, just to make sure the curls are set and defined. Either way, you can finish by misting in some holding spray to fix the look into place. Or, to straighten and smooth, use a volume foam and a flat paddle brush and blow-dry, focusing on making clean, straight lines. The volume foam helps the newly straightened hair retain body and bounce and the round brush blow-dry is a great way to smooth out your hair.

TARA

The Style. Tara's tresses feature natural curl and a fine to thin texture. Again, the problem is giving enough structure and shape to the curls while also creating a vital illusion of thickness for such fine hair. This round two-and-a-half-inch cut really brings out that curly definition while the hairs sit on top of one another to create the appearance of fullness and volume. The bangs help this, too. Soft, loose, and draped effortlessly over Tara's forehead, they add real substance to her style; putting the emphasis across the top of the cut slims down the features of her face. I love how the darkish brown allover single process adds extra definition to her curls, as well. Overall, this is a dynamic way to wear troublesome fine and curly hair.

Stylability. Normally tough-to-manage hair made absolutely easy. All I did was apply a curl-enhancing product to bring out the definition of her curls and a volume foam to disguise any fineness in the hair. No blow-dry; I just cupped and squeezed the curls into a natural formation. A ten-minute job anyone can do.

EMILY

The Style. Emily wears a rounded, layered bob, a great way to add definition to her medium-smooth curly locks *and* in an easy-to-wear way. I scissor-cut this one with lots and lots of layers as an extra way of encouraging these wonderful, shapely curls to come out to play. And lifting the hair away from the face creates a softer, more elegant look. The full head of light brown highlights gives Emily a nice warm color tone and also characterizes the curls. This a polished way for a modern professional to wear full-bodied curly hair.

Stylability. To give Emily extra volume, I applied a curl-enhancing product from roots to ends, gave them a quick squeeze, and then used a diffuser to blow-dry. The diffuser gives an extra jolt of volume and should take no more than fifteen minutes to do. Otherwise, just use your fingers to cup and squeeze the curls while they air-dry, which is perfect for when you need to leave the house in a hurry. If you feel like you need to fix the look in place, a light mist of holding spray will do the job admirably.

ALALEH

The Style. Alaleh has naturally loose and wavy curls, which she used to style straight pretty much every day. That's a lot of work, so I wanted to give her a cut that would play into the movements in her hair. This short, round, graduated razor cut is perfect for her because the curls can be celebrated and it also adds extra fullness and volume, making the curls look full of spring and life. A great way for a professional or a busy mom to wear her curls naturally without too much fuss. And, as you can see, whenever Alaleh wants to go straight, that's easy, too. The straight look was created by using a smoothing lotion with a straightening iron—so simple. For the color, an allover rich, darkish brown single process suits Alaleh's brown eyes and complexion to a tee while also defining the shape of her curls.

Stylability. Because Alaleh's curls are quite loose and susceptible to falling flat, I needed to help them get and hold their shape. I used a curl-promoting product to bring out the curls and a styling crème to help the hair stay set in perfect position. Then I used a curling iron to curl, twist, and shape the curls, with a light mist of holding spray at the end to fix everything into place. This is a great look on the weekend or for a night out, but it may take twenty or thirty minutes to do. For every day, cupping, scrunching, and squeezing your curls with a good dose of curling crème mixed with a styling or setting crème or lotion applied from roots to ends is enough to shape and style your look. Keep a holding spray in your bag and if curls start to droop, mist in a touch of that followed by another round of cupping, scrunching, and squeezing.

VICTORIA

The Style. Victoria's hair is thick and lush, long and curly. Hair like this needs the extra weight to be taken out to create enough space and freedom for the hair to move, especially as Victoria has such amazing natural curls. The classic way to do this is to cut layers into the style. And Victoria's cut is exactly that: a long, heavily layered scissor cut that has a sexy, free-flowing appeal. The layers drape down and across the features of her face, enhancing her natural beauty—a timeless hairstyle that will never go out of fashion. Victoria is a shiny natural brunette, so for the color, I went for a chestnut-toned single process as an easy enhancement to add extra luster.

Stylability. With a style and hair like this you can showcase the natural sheen and smoothness of a straight look or the beautiful natural curly definition. To get the straight look, I applied a styling crème from the roots to the ends, which slicks, sets, and holds the hair, and a defrizz serum from the midlengths to the ends to ease the excess volume that is common in thick and heavy tresses. Then came the blow-dry, in this case on high heat using a large round brush, focusing on smoothing out each section of hair. At the end, there were a few unruly bits and pieces, which is normal for curly heads who are styling their hair straight, so I used a straightening iron to straighten and smooth it out even more. And that was it, done. Thick and curly hair types going for a long, straight style take a few minutes more to style, but the styling done here should take you no more than twenty-five minutes. For a quicker turnaround, Victoria can wear her hair naturally curly and use her curly cowlicks for individuality. To do this I applied a curl-enhancing product and a setting crème to wet hair and cupped, squeezed, and scrunched the curls every fifteen minutes until they were dry.

4. Finding a Hairdresser

When I was a young wannabe hairdresser starting out in the business, I got my first gig as an apprentice in a small salon near my home in Manchester, England. It's true that I was a young creative with plenty of ambition, but to be honest, the real reason I took the job was that I was looking to get paid for listening to music and socializing. Because hair salons are very social places and have music blasting all day, I decided hairdressing was the job for me!

Soon after starting my apprenticeship, I saw an advertisement for assistants for Vidal Sassoon. At the time, Manchester didn't have too many prospects for music-mad teenagers like me. But Vidal Sassoon was an exception. It was the coolest, most glamorous location for any hairdresser north of London. Absolutely brilliant, I thought. Better music and more socializing. I had to apply.

But when I arrived for the interview, the level of professionalism, the commitment to client service, and the quality of the hairdressing struck me hard and true. It was eye-opening and inspiring. The prospects were thrilling. I realized this was my one chance to carve out a successful career and master the art of hairdressing. As for the music and socializing, what a great bonus!

I got the job thanks to the determination I expressed during my interview. And it was there that I learned the foundations of quality haircutting, the importance of a professional consultation, and how essential a great client experience really is.

I'm telling you this because by now you should know what type of hairstyle you'd like (and perhaps even some alternative styles you will want a year—or two—from now), so it's time to give you the tools to find the salon and the hairdresser you need to achieve that look. In a nutshell, the elements of a great salon experience that I learned about as a teenager are just what you should be getting every time you walk into the salon: professionalism, a great consultation, quality cut and color, commitment to the client, and happy staff who take pleasure in their work. If you don't get these things, take your hard-earned dollars to a hair salon that meets all these expectations with an easy, client-friendly smile.

Behind the Chair

Going to the hair salon should be a fun, exciting experience that makes you feel special and rejuvenated, *and* makes you look sensational. Personally, I love being behind the chair and taking care of my clients because it gives me the chance to communicate with people and get them excited about a beautiful, brand-new hairstyle. I can give clients inspiration and the confidence to know that a new look will be right for them. I can find out all their expectations of what they'd like to see at the end of the appointment, adding my own spin to make it an even better look. I give them the haircut they dreamed of, one that I also know they can style easily at home from day to day. Even after twenty-five years in the business, this is an exciting, invigorating experience for me, and you should feel this same passion for hair, this same commitment to understanding your needs, and this same willingness to meet and exceed your expectations, no matter who your hairdresser is.

As in any industry, there are lots of hairdressers who are committed to their craft and continue to try to improve each and every day, and there are hairdressers who haven't had the level of education or experience needed to fulfill all the expectations of their clients. I know who I'd rather have

shaping my personal style. So I'll use my salon experience to give you your best chance of finding the perfect hair salon and the perfect hairdresser for you.

Putting the Process in Order

You can walk into practically any hair salon on any given day and get an appointment. But how much do you really know about the salon and the people working behind the chairs? Most likely, the answer is not a lot. I believe that you should find out everything you possibly can about a salon and its employees before you commit to a cut or color service. To do this, I've broken down the process of finding a salon, and then finding the right hairdresser in that salon,

> Going to the hair salon should be a fun, exciting experience that makes you feel special and rejuvenated, *and* makes you look sensational.

into six easy steps. Some people are nervous about getting their hair made over and others are bold and confident. I can understand both emotions because making a change can be exciting or nerve-racking, depending on your personality and state of mind. However, I encourage everyone to embrace the spirit of change, and the best way to handle any nerves is to arm yourself with as much information as possible, not just about the kind of cut you want and that best suits your hair but also about the best person (and place) for the job.

If you are a bit of a nervous Nellie about getting your hair cut, take this process one step at a time. If you're bold and confident about getting a haircut, and if everything is going according to plan, then you can bundle steps 3 through 6 into one. It's your choice. Many of you already have a hair salon that you visit regularly. That's fine, especially if you've been happy with the results in the past, but I still advise you to take some time to evaluate whether the stylist you have is right for your future and to put him or her to the test by considering some alternatives. I'm not saying you have to change places and people and start all over again, but it's a good idea to use this six-step process as a checklist to make sure you're getting the best cut, color, and experience that you can for your money.

STEP 1: ASK, ASK, ASK

When we see a great piece of architecture, a moving piece of art, or anything new and original that catches our eye, one of the first things that many of us do is find out who created it. To find a great hairdresser, you should do the same. If you see a stranger with Great Hair, be brave and kindly ask her who cut it. I can guarantee that no one will mind the question. Who wouldn't take it as a compliment if a person walked up to her and said, "Oh, my gosh, I absolutely *love* your hair. Where did you get it cut, and who is your stylist?" You can ask friends and family, too, anyone you see or know who appears like-minded, confident, and happy with her look, especially if her hair looks similar to yours in texture and shape and the cut she has is similar to what you want. For example, if you crave a classic cut, ask someone with a great classic cut; if you want an avant-garde cut, ask someone with a great avant-garde cut. Then make a list of every name and place you are referred to.

STEP 2: DO YOUR RESEARCH

Now that you have some referrals to salons and stylists, take advantage of the Information Age in which we are living and find out everything you can about your prospects. It's truly amazing how much you can find out about people and places on the Internet, and this is the perfect place to start to find out more about stylists before you let anyone touch your hair.

To separate the weak from the great, I suggest citysearch.com as your first port of call. It's the best place to judge what real people think because the reviews come from real people who have visited the salon of their own accord. Then those reviews are bundled together by the webmasters to give an average overall rating. It really is the acid test. It's easy to do. Log on to the Web and type in citysearch.com, click on "salons and spas," and you'll find a huge list of places, all in your area. You can read the editorial overview to get a feel for the place and then individual reviews for ratings and personal experiences. Most places score an average of at least 8.5 out of 10. The best places rate above 9.5, so start by looking at the top-rated salons and, if you don't see anything you like, simply work down the list. A word of caution, though: Even the very best salons get the odd bad review—it's the nature of the independent online reviews. Go with the majority, not the minority. Most towns and cities are now covered by citysearch, but if your location isn't, another good idea is to check your local Better Business Bureau. The Better Business Bureau allows consumers to make official, serious complaints only, but because of that, the registered complaints are founded in truth: If the salon you're going to has complaints on the BBB Web site, it's probably best avoided.

You can also use the Web to Google the salon's name. It'll link you to the salon's Web site, or, if it doesn't have a Web site, you should at least be able to find information on the type of work offered and the type of environment. Many salon Web sites now provide biographies of their hairdressers so you can find out a bit more about the experience their employees have, too.

Salons that do have a Web site allow you to discover more about the salon's identity. By clicking around the site you should be able to see whether they only cut or cut and color, whether they just do styling (updo styling salons are becoming increasingly popular), whether they are a full-service spa, whether they have an upbeat, creative feel, whether they are cool and contemporary, or whether they are ornate and refined. You'll also generally find the prices for all their services and the policies of the salon.

Your research should give you a good idea of the salon's identity. Now you can consider where you fit in. Choose a salon that fits well with you and your own idea of what a hair salon should be. What do I mean? Well, if you consider yourself young, contemporary, and cool, then choose a salon whose image reflects the cool and contemporary vibe with which you're most comfortable. Or if you consider yourself to be more conservative and elegant, find a salon with a more classical image to match. If you feel comfortable walking into a salon, it's much more likely that you'll feel comfortable with the experience as a whole.

STEP 3: PEEK IN

Once you've found a few salons that sound good to you, it's time to start getting a feel for them. The next step is to walk by and peek in to get a better feel for what's going on inside the salon, rather than just what's going on in cyberspace.

The first thing to do is look at the stylists and other employees, because if their hair doesn't look great, it's a good bet that the clients aren't looking all that hot, either. At the very least their hair should look clean, healthy, and well cut, but in reality they should be inspiring you with the rich variety of styles, and the quality cut and color of their own hair. And what about their overall image? Do they look like modern beauty professionals? Does their complete image match the expectations you had when you walked into the salon? How does this image fit with you? Ask yourself: "Do I feel comfortable walking in here and letting these people loose on my hair? Are they the right people to shape and define *my* style?"

Next, have a look around the front desk, because this is where the client should be greeted first with professionalism and respect.

You may feel a bit self-conscious walking into a salon just to analyze the place, so come up with a good reason for being there in case anyone asks.

Expect the front desk to be free from overcrowding, staff mumbling among themselves, and general messing around. It definitely should be clean and tidy. If there's lots of staff hanging around, and it feels intimidating to you, it lacks the professionalism you're looking for. Employees should be calm, in control, and welcoming, especially when they see a potential new client.

To firm up your opinion of the salon, look at the clients in the chairs. Are they your type of people? Do they look glad to be there, or desperate to find a way out? Most important: the hair. Check out how finished clients look when they leave the chairs. They should be walking out looking great and happy. Also scrutinize how clean the salon is; it should be immaculate. If it's a mess, it's likely the haircuts will be equally messy.

Finally, look for any in-house promotional material that the salon produces. It doesn't mean it's a bad salon if there isn't anything like in-house newsletters, magazines, press clippings, or their own photo shoots lying around. The salon might not have the time and money for these things. If you do see promotional material, it shows that the owner(s) is trying to push forward, create a brand identity, and connect with the clients, which is always a good thing—and it also enables you, the client, to find out more about the personality of the place where you get your hair done, which is a nice touch for the salon to add. At the very least, there should be a price list for all their services, and you should definitely pop one of those into your bag for future reference.

You may feel a bit self-conscious walking into a salon just to analyze the place, so come up with a good reason for being there in case anyone asks. The best cover is product. All salons sell it, so ask a member of the staff to recommend which products are most suitable for you and your hair. You can say you're looking for something to give you more volume or more hold, or you're looking for a curl-enhancing product, whatever is the best fit for you. (This is

also a good time to ask a professional to define your hair texture and shape.) It gives you a reason to be there and talk to the staff, and a chance to assess how knowledgeable and caring toward potential new clients they are. You might even discover a great new product!

STEP 4: THE BANG TRIM

Another excellent way to gauge a salon and a potential hairdresser is to ask the front desk staff to recommend a stylist to give you a bang trim. This is a five-minute service that is normally complimentary, but check just in case. A bang trim is just what is sounds like: A hairdresser sits you down, sprays some water on your bangs, and trims them so they are tidy, refined, and face framing. If you are asked to pay, it shouldn't be much. But if it's complimentary, it shows that the salon is working hard to build long-term relationships. That's because if you like your bang trim and the way you are treated, then chances are you'll come back. Look for them to be building a relationship with you. Your hairdresser should ask you all the typical getting-to-know-you questions: What's your name? Where are you from? What do you do? How do you like your hair? How short would you like your bangs? and so on and so forth. Remember to analyze your hairdresser. Is he or she calm and confident? Do you feel comfortable and relaxed? If the hairdresser can't manage a bang trim without making you nervous, you know not to go back for a complete cut. On the other hand, if he or she makes your bangs look great, and impresses you with an air of confidence,

knowledge, and skill, you can start thinking about making an appointment.

STEP 5: MAKE YOUR APPOINTMENT

If you were happy with your bang trim, you may want to go straight to the front desk and book an appointment with that stylist. If you want more time to mull it over, just say "thank you" and "I'll call to make an appointment"—easy. However, if you skipped over the bang trim (or you don't have bangs!) or are still unsure, how can you be sure you are choosing the right hairdresser for you?

With all my experience, I can safely say the best hairdressers are, regardless of how much they charge, the busiest hairdressers. When you call to make an appointment, it's a good idea to ask the front desk who are the busiest, most popular stylists. Normally, if you let the front-desk team lead the conversation and recommend a stylist to you, they will refer you to the least busy stylist because it's the quieter ones who have the most open slots. I don't believe in this policy, and it's certainly not one I employ, but most salons do, so be forceful and make sure you get the stylist you want.

Another way to ensure you get a great hairdresser is the price. Of course a high price is no guarantee of high quality, but the more expensive stylists usually have more experience, and if they charge a lot and still retain a strong client base, then they must be doing something right.

If you're looking for a cheaper option, many

salons have great educational programs for apprentice hairdressers. These youngsters may indeed have exceptional skill and training but simply lack the experience they need to merit charging higher prices. When you call, ask what training, if any, younger, less experienced stylists are given. If the salon has a good education program and makes a habit of hiring talented, creative, and driven young stylists, then it's a fantastic low-cost option.

STEP 6: THE CONSULTATION

If you're still not ready to take the plunge, call and ask for an appointment for a consultation. Say something like, "I'm thinking about getting my hair cut but I'm not sure how. Could I set up a consultation so I can get a better idea about what options I have?" Again, that's easy. If you do go ahead and book an appointment to get your hair cut, then your appointment should also start with a consultation.

This is where you can really see how good a stylist someone is, because a hairdresser's consultation skills are critical. For a hairdresser, the ability to communicate with a client is fundamental. When I conduct a consultation, the first thing I do is listen and understand what my client wants—what are her expectations? Expect any hairdresser worth his or her salt to do the same, because a hairdresser who doesn't understand your expectations has zero chance of matching—let alone exceeding—them.

So make sure that after the introductions your stylist is listening to you. Tell your hairdresser what you expect to happen, and be

specific: Do you want to take an inch off the bottom, or five inches? Do you want a strong shape or a soft shape? Do you want layers or graduation? A textured, messy look? A long smooth, polished cut?

This is also the time to show your hairdresser any hairstyle pictures you have found in this book, in magazines, or anywhere else. Definitely don't hesitate to take a picture or two to show off what you want. Hairdressers are visual, creative people and generally respond well to a visual example. One note of caution: Choose a picture for the hair, not for the image of the person. The image is likely manufactured; the hair is real. Focus on the haircut and how that's going to work for you day to day rather than trying to look like the airbrushed celebrity or model does in that one moment in time.

After about two minutes of my clients talking to me about their expectations and showing me any pictures of styles they'd like to go for, I take up the reins by telling them the truth—that what they want is a great fit for them or that the style they envision isn't quite right. If what they want is a good fit, I push things forward a bit by suggesting a few exciting or trend-conscious ideas of my own that I believe will work great on the individual in question. If I don't think a style is right, I quickly explain why, to keep the confidence of my client. It may be that the hair texture and shape just don't suit what she wants to achieve; it may be that the hair is damaged and needs to be cut in a way that will make it damage-free; or it may be that the style is so difficult to achieve day to day that I feel it is too much work for the person.

Check Yourself Out

You should perform two self-checks to make sure your expectations are reasonable. What do I mean? Well, if you are making your consultation last more than ten minutes, then you are asking a lot of your hairdresser. It may be that you are struggling to give up the reins. You need to have confidence in the professional and learn to enjoy the process of change. (Of course, if it's your hairdresser who is taking more than ten minutes, you know he or she lacks self-confidence.) Second, if you've tried peeking in five or more salons without feeling comfortable in any one of them, then again you may be struggling to commit to a new cut. Be brave, choose your favorite of the five (or more), and enjoy being pampered and transformed into a beautiful new you.

Whatever the reason, it is then my job to offer some alternatives and get the client excited about what those suggestions can—and will—do for her. Obviously, all hairdressers have their own way of expressing themselves and their own patterns of thought, but expect your stylist to be honest with you and to take the time to explain what he or she thinks, whatever that is. Your stylist should have good, creative ideas of his or her own as well as an awareness of any potential problems.

If the stylist foresees any problems, you should certainly listen to what he or she has to say. If your stylist is able to give you concrete reasons as to why the style you want won't work for you, you should consider his or her opinion and appreciate that he or she is looking out for your best interests. On the other hand, if your stylist can't reasonably explain why a particular style isn't right for you, then you would be wise to walk away.

When your hairdresser takes up the reins, listen carefully and determine if he or she has listened to and understood your expectations. If the stylist has any exciting or trend-savvy ideas, decide whether *you* like the suggestions. You're looking for someone with good communication skills, knowledge, confidence, and creativity. If your stylist exhibits those qualities and you're feeling confident and excited about the ideas you've exchanged, then, great, you're in good

shape and can commit to a cut. If you're unsure, you can say thank you for the consultation and the ideas, but you'd like to think about it before

> f your stylist is able to give you concrete reasons as to why the style you want won't work for you, you should consider his or her opinion.

making a decision. If your hairdresser has a visible lack of confidence, no matter what the situation, you should walk away. Done right, a consultation truly allows you to assess whether you have found the right chair.

If you like your hairdresser but are perhaps concerned with what he or she wants to do, or the responses you've gotten to your questions, then do ask for a second, more experienced, opinion. The stylist should be calm and comfortable with this request. If not, it's a sign you're in the wrong hands. It shouldn't be a problem to say, "Hey, I like your ideas, but can we get a second opinion just to make sure we're going in the right direction?" At that point you should expect the owner, director, or manager to step in and give you the answers you want. In no more than two or three minutes he or she should reassure you that your hairdresser is doing the right thing, or make a new, improved suggestion and explain why the original idea

wasn't quite right. At that point you can quickly assess again whether you're in the right chair.

On the flip side, hairdressers occasionally invite a second opinion themselves. Don't let this worry you. It shows they care enough to make sure they're doing the right thing. Especially for a young stylist, this is a brave and sensible move. Leaning on the experience of a senior colleague is something I ask all my young stylists to do.

The Cut

If you're comfortable and happy with the stylist you've found using the six steps, get the cut and give a big warm welcome to a beautiful brand-new you. Remember, your hairdresser is there for you. Make sure your hairdresser helps you feel good about yourself and makes you look polished, sensational, and sexy. And, unless you've asked for something different, make sure you get a cut that you can style easily at home day to day. As I mentioned, a good haircut lasts a minimum of six weeks before the style starts to fail. How long the style lasts is another great way to tell if the cut you get is truly a good one. Most stylists can style your hair to look good by the end of your appointment, but if after three or four weeks it's starting to look lifeless and limp, you know the foundations of the haircut weren't right. If this is the case for you, speak to your hairdresser about putting that right. If he or she can't fix the problem, my advice is to go to somebody who can.

BUILDING A RELATIONSHIP

If you want Great Hair, build a great relationship with your hairdresser. Don't expect a one-hit wonder. Think about it: When you're out and about and you meet someone new, the first conversations are made up of small talk. It's always better the second time around. It's the same for a hairdresser. The first time we're getting to know you and your expectations, as well as the makeup of your hair. Finding a hairdresser you feel comfortable with and building a relationship allow you to work together for the long-term health, integrity, and style of your hair, and that's much better than yo-yoing from hairdresser to hairdresser.

THE RAZOR

Nowadays more and more hairdressers are cutting with a razor instead of scissors. Personally, I love the razor and use it a lot. I find it's an excellent way to create modern, low-maintenance hairstyles. If you've had, or get, a bad razor cut, don't automatically think it's the razor's fault. You may have been to

Curl Conscious

Many curly-haired people let only another curly-haired person cut their hair! The belief is you have to have curly hair to understand curly hair. Rubbish. Just because you have curly hair doesn't mean you know how to cut it. If you have curly hair, your focus should be the same as any other hair type: Get a great hairdresser. A great hairdresser can cut any hair shape or texture into a style-defining look you'll love.

a substandard hairdresser who didn't know how to use the razor correctly. Anyone proficient in both tools knows you can manipulate a razor to do anything you can do with scissors, and vice versa. It comes down to the hairdresser's personal preference. But to give you a better idea of why your hairdresser chooses a razor over scissors, let's take a quick look at some of the uses for this great tool.

- Enables swing and movement
- Creates a modern, jagged line
- Gives the freedom to redefine hair texture(s)

- Thins out thick hair
- Creates a short, messy, and shaggy hairstyle
- Makes beautiful, soft, shaped layers

Speaking Our Language

We hairdressers often use technical terms like "texturizing" or "undercutting" when talking to you in a consultation. It's our way of explaining what we want to achieve in the haircut. I know this hairdresserspeak can be a bit of a mind boggle and leave you wondering just what it is that we're up to. So I'll finish this chapter with a look at what all this fancy technical terminology really means for you.

Texturizing (sometimes called "point cutting") removes weight or bulk within the shape and structure of the haircut. Your hairdresser thins out the lower portion of your hair (or even just the very ends) almost strand for strand for a softer, lighter look with lots of movement, giving tailored fluidity and pieciness to the haircut. It's also a common technique to define short, loose, and messy textures.

Graduation is a classic haircutting technique where the hair is tapered into the nape of your neck. It's a subtle and gradual buildup of weight to add strength to the style of the cut, and it is often used to soften a one-length line so it doesn't appear so severe.

Layering removes weight and bulkiness by cutting much shorter pieces that fall above your desired length. Instead of your hair being all one length, the cut is layered to create tiers of hair around the shape of the face, adding texture and curves, looseness and freedom.

Hairdressers often say "I'm going to get your hair to swing and move." This can be done with any number of cuts and means that they're looking to create space and freedom in your

haircut to allow your hair to swing and move freely and sexily. For example, a layered haircut has a lot more freedom and movement than a one-length cut.

When hairdressers says they'll be cutting a one-length line, they are going for the strongest possible perimeter shape. Rather than cutting in layers or texturizing the interior, all your hair will reach the same length. It doesn't have the same softness and movement as some other haircuts, but it provides a strong, solid structure for you to work with.

If you have thick, bulky hair, it's likely your hairdresser will take some of the weight out. Literally, this means that he or she cuts the interior (rather than the exterior shape) of the hair to remove bulky, unnecessary pieces. This can also be explained as "thinning out" the hair.

Undercutting makes your hair livelier and fuller by cutting the hair underneath shorter than the top layers. It allows the hair to fall effortlessly into place, creating a support structure for your style, and gives the illusion of extra body and bounce.

Summing It All Up

This chapter gives you the tools to find the right salon and the right hairdresser for you. Find a salon that is committed to professionalism, client service, and quality hairdressing, and you're well on your way to a great hairstyle. Be mindful that choosing a salon that matches your own image and your own expectations of how a hair salon should be gives you your best chance of feeling comfortable when you put your trust in it to revamp your style.

My six-step process to finding the right salon and hairdresser is a guide to help you on your journey; use it any way that works for you. But pay particular attention to my thoughts on the consultation: By gauging a hairdresser's communication skills in the consultation you get a great idea of how good the stylist truly is. And

this is the last chance you have (before the cut) to walk away if you don't feel like you're in the right hands. Remember, too, that this chapter shows you how to evaluate the quality of your haircut up to six weeks after the event. The guide to the benefits of razor cutting should help you understand why it has become such a popular way to cut hair—it's a great modern option that creates a lot of versatility, movement, and freedom in your hairstyle.

I also encourage you to build a great relationship with your hairdresser. Find a stylist you like and work together for the long-term benefit of your hair. This is a much more progressive approach than trying a new hairdresser every time you need a haircut (although, of course, if your stylist and/or salon fails to fulfill your expectations, you can look around for somewhere and someone that will).

5. Styling at Home

Creating salon-perfect hair at home requires following a few simple rules and a few basic techniques. I hope in the previous chapters you learned those golden rules: Work *with* your hair, be realistic about what your hair can achieve and what it cannot, pick a few styles that you love and that are right for you and your lifestyle, and subtly change your hair's style and color every so often to look modern and youthful all the time.

With the help of this book, you should now have the right hairstyle. You've gone to the salon, you got a great cut, and your stylist blew it out beautifully. You felt fabulous. Then you went home. And the next morning, after you washed it, you couldn't re-create that style. Your stylist made it look so easy, even gave you a so-called low-maintenance do. But it's not low maintenance to you. What now?

This chapter teaches you how to do all those salon styling tricks right at your vanity table. You'll end up looking and feeling just as if you were stepping out of the salon chair with ultrafab hair every day.

I recommend reading all the styling techniques in this chapter, even if there are some you think you'll never want or need. That way you'll get a feeling for the consistencies that run through all hair styling and a feeling for the subtle variations that create different looks.

I cover everything from the basic blow-out technique for long and short hair to volumizing, dealing with frizz, and options for both curly and straight hair. Then I pump it up a notch, working on some exciting updos. So grab a brush and let's begin.

Tools of the Trade

Without a brush, a blow-dryer, or products, you simply can't manipulate your hair into the various styles showcased in this chapter. All hairstylists, no matter how great they are, are powerless if they don't have tools to work with. So let's go through the user-friendly, at-a-glance tables of the different products and tools at your disposal. You'll find more in-depth descriptions as you go through this chapter, but these two tables should get you started and function as a great reference guide as you move forward.

For almost everything you want to do, you need to apply a preparation product to damp hair before you blow-dry and then, after the blow-dry, you need a finishing product to add the final, individual details to your look. There are lots of preparation and finishing products to choose from. Some are more suited to certain hair types, but all do a good job provided you apply them correctly. It's just a matter of finding the ones that achieve the looks you want and work best with your hair.

Products

Product	Preparation or Finish?	Hair Types	Purpose	How to Use
Holding spray	Finish	All hair types	Long-lasting hold and control	Hold 6–8 inches from head and spray directly onto hair.
Thermal protector	Preparation	Any hair that is having a heat tool applied	Foundation for any type of do and essential heat protection	Apply evenly through damp hair from roots to ends before using heat tools and styling products.
Styling crème	Preparation	All hair types	A volumizing base to support, slick, set, and hold	Work evenly through damp hair to set and style or blow-dry in for extra fullness.
Volume foam	Preparation	All hair types and especially limp or lifeless hair	Lift, thickness, and support, no matter your hairstyle	Focus product at the root, distributing evenly through to the midsection of the hair shaft.
Blow-dry setting spray	Preparation	All hair in need of a blow-dry	Beautiful blow outs	Spray evenly onto damp hair before your blow out, making sure to get product in at the roots.
Mousse	Preparation	All hair types	Hold, control, and uplifting volume	Apply from roots to the midsection on damp hair before you blow-dry.
Defrizz serum	Preparation and finish	Frizzy hair, curly hair that wants to be straight	Eliminate frizz and flyaways	Place a few drops on palms and work through midsection and ends before blow-drying frizz away.

Product	Preparation or Finish?	Hair Types	Purpose	How to Use
Gel	Preparation and finish	All hair types	To slick, set, and hold	For maximum hold and control, rub into palms, work through damp hair, and blow dry. For a softer style, push through damp hair and air dry.
Hair crème	Finish	All hair types	A smoothed-out, natural finish or a sexy slept-in look	Work it in from root to tip and blow-dry smooth or air dry.
Curl crème	Preparation and finish	Curly and frizzy hair	Luscious curls and frizz-free looks	Apply evenly to damp hair, from roots to ends, then gently squeeze curls and finger-style.
Texture paste, pomade, or wax (they all work in a very similar way)	Finish	All hair, but best on short and/or messy styles	Texture and separation with a smooth matte finish	Rub a nickel-sized dab into palms and work through midsection and ends of damp hair.
Leave-in conditioner	Finish	All hair types	A healthy, polished finish or a soft curl	Use fingers or a comb to work a liberal amount evenly through damp hair.
Shine spray	Finish	Any hair you want to glisten	Soft sheen to finish a blow-dry	Spray drops into hand and work through ends of blown-out hair.

Tools and Brushes

Tool or Brush	Hair Types	Purpose	How to Use
Blow-dryer	All hair, except the super-super short	Take away hair's excess moisture; create your own individual hairstyle	Hold 6"–8" away from head and keep dryer moving to avoid overdried patches.
Nozzle	All hair types	A focused blow-dry, with the heat going where it's needed most	Attach nozzle to dryer and dry as desired.
Diffuser	Curly hair	Beautiful, polished curls	Attach diffuser to dryer and dry curls at roots.
Curling iron	All hair types, but don't use on dry, damaged, and overprocessed hair	Create natural-looking curls and waves in straight hair	Wrap iron around hair to create curl; the more you wrap, the more curl you create.
Flat iron	Curly or wavy types, but don't use on dry, damaged, and overprocessed hair	Straighten hair and give it a polished finish	Work from the underneath up in sections all across hair, especially on unruly waves you want to eliminate.
Small round bristle brush (1" diameter)	All straight hair types, but most effective on shorter styles	Add lift and volume to short hair, create tight and curly ringlets; smooth out hair	Use the roundness and the bristles to give roots lift as you blow-dry or wrap hair around the brush as you dry for tight ringlets.
Medium round bristle brush (1½"–2½" diameter)	All straight hair types	Layer in lift and volume; create soft waves or curls	Use with dryer to lift hair away from the roots or wrap hair around brush as you dry for loose waves and curls.

Tool or Brush	Hair Types	Purpose	How to Use
Big round bristle brush (2½" diameter)	All straight hair types, but most effective on superthick and/or superlong hair	Add volume or to create big, loose waves	Use with dryer to lift hair away from the roots or wrap hair around brush as you dry for superloose waves.
Flat paddle brush	All hair types except extremely curly textures	Smooth out unwanted waves or curls; also for creating volume	Use with dryer, working from the underneath up to create desired effect.
Vent brush	All hair but especially good for shorter styles	Manage a fast blow-dry and manipulate hair as desired	Use with dryer, working from the underneath up to create desired effect; let the heat of dryer pass through vents of brush.
Wide-tooth comb	All hair types but especially curly textures	Evenly distribute product in your hair	Apply product and comb evenly throughout.
Your hands and fingers	All hair types	Finish your style and add a touch of playful messiness	Run fingers loosely through damp or dry hair and style as desired.

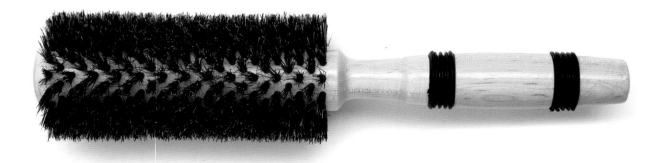

Blow-Out Basics

Unless your hair is supershort, you have to blow it dry in some fashion. Not only is it easy, it's also the foundation from which to build a variety of wonderful hairstyles—what's added are salon techniques for you to manipulate, control, and style your hair any way you wish. You have to learn to blow-dry correctly to guarantee smoothness and prevent roughing of the cuticle. Blow-dry with the wrong technique and you're likely to create frizz and flyaways. Following are the guiding principles of a great blow out.

1. **You need a good dryer with plenty of heat.** Whether you want to smooth, mold, straighten, set, or defrizz, it's the heat that does the work, locking in the desired texture and finish for your look. Your dryer should have at least 1,200 watts of heat and come with a nozzle. This should cost you about $40. You can find dryers with up to 2,000 watts. These dry the hair much faster, but they cost more. Expect to pay over $100 for a high-powered dryer. Anytime you blow-dry your hair, it's essential to use a nozzle. This simple attachment allows the airflow to penetrate the hair shaft, giving greater, more focused control for styling. Hairdressers call this "directional blow styling," and it's fundamental for the success of any blow-dry.

2. **Remove most of the water in your hair with a towel prior to blow-drying.** Never apply product or attempt to blow out hair when you can still squeeze out excess water. If, after towel drying, your hair is still dripping wet, use your dryer to evenly remove excess moisture. Stop when your hair is still damp so that you can apply your foundation product at that critical stage. This ensures that the product penetrates the hair shaft and can reach its full potential. If you miss this sweet spot, the product will never be as effective.

3. **Always blow-dry from roots to ends.** Start at the roots, moving gently along the hair shaft, and finish at the hair tip. You do this with a brush and a blow-dryer. The brush always comes first, with the dryer following the path set out by the brush. Hold the dryer about six to ten inches away from your head. If you're burning your scalp, it's too close; if you can't feel any heat on your head, it's too far away.

4. Begin by lifting up your hair and placing the brush underneath, at the roots of the hair. Take only sections of hair that are small enough for you to grasp, manage, and control. Hold the dryer over the brush and hair, following its root-to-tip path, covering the same section of hair, in exactly the same direction as the brush. Work each section until dry; this should take no more than two or three goes for each section.

5. Every dryer has a cool-shot button; this fixes and finishes your look and must be used wisely. Heat molds and manipulates as desired, but hair is never really fixed into place until it's cool to the touch. So make sure you cool-blast after every blow-dry. This locks in the finish on your hair, preventing your style from fading as the day wears on.

BLOW-DRYING A BOB

The best thing about a bob is the swing and movement you can create with a good blow-dry. This shows off its beauty—timeless, classic, and always in. To achieve this in your own blow-dry, use the first technique I was ever taught, the wraparound blow-dry. Here it is, step by step.

1. On damp hair, apply a foundation product. Volumizing foam, a blow-dry setting spray, or a thickening spray are all good foundation products and work perfectly.

2. Now, with the nozzle attached, blow-dry your hair, ideally using a flat paddle brush, to literally wrap your hair around and around your scalp.

3. I'll explain this in its simplest terms: As you blow-dry, start with the brush placed on your hair just above the top of your forehead, where the roots from your bangs begin. Keep the brush on your scalp and literally brush it all the way around your head. From the front, go 360 degrees around your head. Go through one side of your hair, then through the back, and around the other side to its starting point, with the heat of the dryer following the path set out by the brush. Now do the exact same thing going in the other direction.

4. Repeat this process over and again, back and forth, back and forth, back and forth. Really work it—it's the best way to create the swing you want.

5. To avoid the little bit of fuzz and frizz in the texture that often comes with this technique, stop the wraparound dry when your hair is about 95 percent dry. Then go through section by section, panel by panel, and blow-dry from the underneath up. Make sure you blast the underneath nice and flat, especially if your hair is thick or wavy. This prevents any little waves or wiggles at the root from coming back to haunt you throughout the day.

6. If you're confident you've followed step 5 correctly but still find some waves underneath, you can replace the brush and dryer with a straightening iron (see page 111 for details). The heat of the iron straightens out the most unruly hair.

If you have short hair, great; it's easier to manage, modern, and sexy. But successful styling depends mostly on the quality of the cut. Why? Because a short shape is structured—balance, proportion, and simplicity are key, so you really must have a great cut. If you need bags of product to create shape, then, quite simply, the cut isn't good enough. Also, too much product in short hair makes it look crispy, dated, and old-fashioned. Short hair should be soft to touch and easy to run your hands through—so go easy on the gel and even easier on the hair or holding spray.

Use Your Head
The Wonders of the Wraparound Blow-Dry

This technique allows you to do many different things. Want smoother hair? Women have been wrapping up their hair before bedtime for centuries (ask your grandmother!) to create smoothness. You're not going to do that, but I will give you some ideas to create smoothness, lift, and body with the wraparound technique, no matter what your hair type.

First of all, remember your head is round, not flat, so if you want lift, smoothness, and body, you can use the natural rounded smoothness of your scalp. To recap: As always, towel-dry most of the moisture away and apply some foundation product. Then take your brush (a paddle brush is best because its shape also encourages smoothness) and blow-dry your hair from the front all the way around, 360 degrees in one direction, with the heat of the dryer following your brush, and then repeat, going the opposite way, repeat, repeat, and repeat till dry. Have fun with it, going from side to side, and round and round. All that wrapping around a rounded surface creates roundness—now you have shape with natural body and lift. Because heat smoothes and your scalp and skull are smooth, too, you've also blown in smoothness. It's a simple and effective technique anybody can do.

Whatever your style, long or short, I urge you to try this technique. For example, if you have curly or wavy hair and want to straighten it out while creating some smoothness, you can use your brush and dryer as in the smooth blow out (see page 109), or you can try the wraparound. Done correctly, both work, but this book is all about giving you the options and the tools to control your hair. Try them both and discover which works better for you.

BLOW-DRYING SHORT HAIR WITH A BRUSH

It's quick, easy, and effective.

1. A vent brush is the ideal tool for blow-drying short hair because the air vents in the brush allow the heat of the dryer to pass quickly into your hair. Some women, however, feel more comfortable with a small round brush. If that's you, no problem, but be extracautious not to wrap your hair around the brush, as this will cause a bubble effect in your hairstyle (see page 104).

2. Your prep product should be a styling crème, a volume foam, or a mousse. But remember, you need only a little for short hair, and make sure to distribute evenly.

3. Because short hair is so cropped, it needs lift at the roots to give it some striking definition. So you're aiming to create height at the crown by lifting this area with your brush as you dry. (Your crown, by the way, is the central point of your head, the top of the skull, where the shape and root direction of your hair begin.) With the nozzle attached, blow-dry each section as you lift up and away with your brush. Remember, with short hair the sections dry much faster, so each section should require only one or two good blasts of heat, and, to ensure you don't overdry one particular section, it's a good idea to keep the dryer moving throughout.

4. Now use the same technique all across your head. It'll give your short hair some bounce, some lift, and tons of style.

5. When your hair is dry, you can use a finishing product—a pomade or texture paste will do fine—to create your individual and polished style. Just remember to distribute your chosen product evenly from the underneath, up and through the hair shaft, and all the way to the ends for any final detailing you want to add. Try slicking it back, messing it up, or anything else you think would be fun.

The Round Brush
Beware of the Bubble

The round brush is the most common brush. It's easy to use and easy to learn about; it's also good for creating volume and for grabbing hair nice and tight for smoothness.

But it does present a big challenge, a misdemeanor I see almost every day: the bubble effect. Common in bangs and short hair, the bubble effect occurs when the hair has been wrapped around the full circumference of a round brush and blow-dried in an attempt to create volume. The result is a rounded sausage shape and, worse, the hair rolls underneath itself, looking turned under, heavily forced, unattractive, and old-fashioned.

Yes, you want lift at your roots, and especially in your bangs (so your hair doesn't fall flat on your forehead), but you definitely don't want the bubble effect.

The round brush is specifically designed for easy access to the roots of your hair. Take advantage of its functionality; instead of wrapping hair around the brush, place the brush in at the roots and brush from the underneath up, from roots to ends, with the heat of the dryer following exactly the same path. This is a much more effective method of creating volume. For more on this technique, check out the volumizing section on page 107 for all the details you need. And again, if you're trying to create smoothness, the smooth blow-out section of this chapter showcases the best way to use the round brush without any danger of the bubble.

BLOW-DRYING SHORT HAIR WITH YOUR FINGERS

With a short cut, product, a dryer, and your fingers may be all the styling tools you need. Don't underestimate the power of your hands to manipulate and control your blow-dry.

1. On damp hair, apply a little foundation product. Styling crème is great for short hair, but volume foam or mousse works, too.

2. Now simply use your fingers to pull your hair up and away from your scalp, nice and taut; this gives you the life and bounce you want. Now, with the nozzle attached, use your blow-dryer to apply some heat. Again, with short hair, the

sections dry much faster, so keep the dryer moving; each section should require only one or two good blasts of heat.

3. Be careful not to overdry one particular area. Short hair dries very fast, and drying a section too quickly creates unwanted and unsightly blow-dry marks. Be sure to keep your fingers and dryer moving across the front, back, and side sections, and you'll have nothing to worry about.

4. For the finish, pomade or texture paste is perfect for creating your own individual, polished style. Just remember to distribute your chosen product evenly from the underneath, up the hair shaft, and finally through to your ends for any final detailing you want to add.

VOLUMIZING

Now you've learned the basic blow out and the ins and outs of shorter hair. But if your hair is longer, there's so much more you can do to achieve your own individual style. Let's talk about blow-drying for extra body and lift, awesome for giving longer-hair types a great boost. Because longer hair carries more weight than, say, short crop cuts, you need to build volume, with product and heat from the roots. This way you maintain full-bodied volume all day, and most of the night as well, even in the longest, thickest, and heaviest hair. The technique is simple, just some small variations from the basic blow out.

1. **The right product is the key ingredient for creating volume.** You need a body-building product—mousse, volume foam, thickening spray, or light gel all work, but my favorite is foam. It's light to the touch and easy to apply because of its airy consistency. And remember: The more product you use, the more you volumize your hair.

2. **On damp, towel-dried hair, apply the product at your roots.** You can work through to the midsection—halfway up the hair shaft—to help evenly distribute product, but it's at the root where you need to focus the product because this is where volume succeeds or fails. How much product depends on how much hair; experiment to see what works best for you, but a dime-sized dollop is the minimum you need. Start with this

amount; you can always add more if you think you need it.

3. Now it's time to blow-dry in some volume. The best brush is a medium-sized round brush or a paddle brush—unless your hair is really long. Then you should use a larger diameter round brush, as it will naturally help lift hair away from the scalp.

4. In easy-to-manage sections, brush your roots up, up, and away from the scalp. Point the dryer at your hair from underneath and follow the path of the brush. Do this at the back, on the sides, or on top—anywhere you want fullness. This creates volume by drying your hair away from your roots, while the already applied product holds your newfound volume in place.

5. Remember, you're focusing on lifting the roots from the scalp, but be sure to blow-dry through to the tips of the hair shaft so your hair dries evenly.

6. Sometimes it is easier to achieve the desired result if you blow-dry your hair with your head down. Bend your head and allow your hair to fall a full 90 degrees and blow-dry according to the principles set out in step 4. This method makes it easier to get at the roots of your hair.

7. Be sure to cool-blast your hair so it's fixed and set into place. This locks in your volume, stopping it from fading throughout the day.

FRIZZ FACTOR PART 1: THE SMOOTH BLOW OUT

Many women suffer from frizz, yet few actually have frizzy hair. So what is this frizz factor that's consumed so many product dollars? Natural frizz comes only if you have coarse, wiry, extra-thick, or extra dry hair (not many of us at all, and I address those issues in Chapter 7, "Problem Hair and Maintenance"). However, if you have naturally curly or wavy medium to thick hair or finer, more fragile hair and you're trying to make it smooth or straight, the problem is the frizz-inducing conflict forged in this straightening process. Step by step, let's look at how to combat frizz while smoothing and straightening your hair.

1. The first step in fighting frizz is to keep hair in tip-top shape. Clean and healthy hair is much easier to control. (See page 175 for more details on how to maintain gorgeous, healthy hair.)

2. The next step is using the right product. For medium to thick hair types, you need only one product—a defrizz serum. Use a good amount, a dime-sized at least. On damp hair, use your fingers to distribute evenly from the midsection of the hair shaft through to the tips of each and every piece of hair. There's no need to apply the serum at the roots. Roots and scalp are always healthier than the mid-section and tips, and are not prone to frizz.

3. If your hair is finer and more fragile, you need two products. First, use a body-building product like a volume foam,

followed by a *very small amount* of defrizz serum; too much serum on fine hair weighs it down and makes it look greasy. Apply the foam at the roots and work it through all of your hair, right through to the tips. But apply the serum only from the midsection—halfway up the hair shaft—to the ends.

4. Smoothing crèmes and lotions are newer products. These are used in exactly the same way as defrizz serum. They can, however, leave a little moisture, and consequently oil, in your hair, so keep well away from the scalp—no defrizz product is needed near the scalp because it's always healthier.

5. Now that your product(s) is evenly applied in the right places, blow-dry on a high heat using a round bristle brush. The technique is the same as the basic blow-dry: from roots to ends in small, easy-to-manage sections, with the bristle brush leading and the heat of the dryer following exactly the same root-to-tip path set out by the brush. This straightens and smoothes your hair to your heart's content and still stops all frizz. Go over each section until dry. Typically this takes two or three repeat applications of brush and dryer.

6. The technique is successful because the bristles of the brush hold your hair smooth while the product's silicone ingredient works together with the high heat of the dryer as an extra source of smoothness.

Flat Iron Forward

Nowadays there are a number of different flat iron options on the market, from the very narrow 1" version to the very wide 3" irons. Wide flat irons are designed for thick, heavy, and long hair, whereas the narrow version is more versatile and great at getting in tricky places such as your bangs or behind the ears. Unless your hair really is superthick and superlong, I recommend using something around 1½"; this size can do most things and is easier to manipulate. I also recommend purchasing an iron with a built-in thermometer gauge, which allows you to control the amount of heat applied to your hair. You can buy a good-quality ceramic flatiron for around $40.

The flat iron technique for straightening hair is almost identical to the standard dryer-and-brush method just outlined, but you need a change of product. Your foundation product is now a thermal protector, which protects your hair from the inevitable stress from the iron's heat and works just fine for your foundation. At this point (just before you use the flat iron), you can apply a little hairspray or even a drop of shine spray. Both help to press your hair flat. The shine spray gives you more sheen and the hairspray makes hair super-superflat. That's your choice.

Once you apply your products thoroughly from roots to ends, you can use the flat iron in the same way you'd use the dryer and a brush, working from the underneath up, section by section, all across your head. There are just a couple of things you should remember: Don't clamp the iron onto your hair. Holding all that heat in one place is sure to burn, break, and damage even the strongest hair. Instead, learn to iron each section quickly and effectively by keeping the iron moving gently and evenly down the hair shaft. Finally, after your ironing out is complete, it's a good idea to blast your hair with a cool shot of air from your blow-dryer (there's no cool-shot button on

flat irons). As you now know, this helps to set your hair in place.

Naturally, an iron is easy to work with because instead of combining two tools (a brush and a dryer), you need only one—and an extremely effective one, at that. As with a curling iron, I highly recommend you invest in a top-quality moisturizing conditioner to put back the moisture lost when using all that heat.

FRIZZ FACTOR PART 2: CONTROLLED CURLS

What if you've got curly or wavy hair and would love some lush, healthy curls without the frizz natural curls can create? Here's your answer.

1. **Product, product, product.** Use enough of the right product at the right time with the right technique and I guarantee you'll create beautiful curls and eliminate frizz. The product locks your curls together and helps you create what I call a natural wet set.

2. For this you need two products. If your hair is fine, use a body-building foam or mousse first and then a curl crème or leave-in conditioner. If your hair is medium to thick or slightly coarse, use a gel or styling crème first, followed by a defrizz serum.

3. For this technique you don't need to blow-dry your hair; instead, towel-dry but leave your hair damp to aid distribution and saturation of the products.

4. Apply the first product, working in from the underneath up, from roots to ends. Again, a dime-sized dollop should do; just make sure to start at the roots and work through to the tip, distributing evenly as you go.

5. Apply the second product in exactly the same way, from roots to ends, distributing evenly.

6. Now comb evenly and gently with a wide-tooth comb. This loosens any knots in your hair and further aids the even distribution of the products, ensuring your curls get their maximum performance benefits.

7. Once you have evenly distributed the two products, use your fingers to squeeze each and every section of your hair. This encourages a natural curl formation. It's best to lean over, letting your hair fall 90 degrees to the ground, while squeezing *gently* with your fingers. You are not squeezing a stress ball! Rather, cup the curl in your hand and gently squeeze and push the curl back into itself with no pressure at the root. Don't be tempted to run your fingers freely through your hair—this only disturbs the

curls you've created and induces frizz. Cup and squeeze, cup and squeeze, cup and squeeze.

8. Once done, leave your hair alone for fifteen minutes and then squeeze again using exactly the same technique. Repeat this process until dry. If you have to run out the door, not to worry; it's a myth that you shouldn't leave the house with wet hair. You can still squeeze hair in the car, on the train, or anywhere else, for that matter—the results will still be the same, although it might be better to do it with your head upright, instead of facing downward as recommended in step 7!

9. When your curls are dry, you will most likely find them set in a slightly crisp formation. This is normal and nothing to worry about. You can now use your fingers to tousle out and ruffle your roots to develop the softer, looser curls you're after. To do this, place your fingertips gently into your roots and massage, using just the very tips of your fingertips in short strokes. Don't disturb the ends by raking your fingers all over your hair. Again, this disturbs the curl formation you've worked to create, inducing frizz in the process. There are about five hundred hairs to every curl, and the idea is to keep those five hundred hairs locked together for brilliant curly definition—carelessly running your fingers through your hair is guaranteed to pull those beautiful curls apart.

10. Don't worry about your curls being even—they're not supposed to be. Curls are as individual as you or I and are meant to fall imperfectly. Enjoy this newfound freedom and uniqueness.

11. For added definition and hold, you can lightly spritz with a nonaerosol holding spray. This locks in your curls throughout the day.

CREATING CURL

Moving on to a slightly more advanced technique: What if you have straight hair and would love some sexy curls or waves to enhance your look? The good news is that curls are easy to craft if you know how. But your hair does need a little length, approaching your shoulders at least.

1. You need a midsized round brush (go for a larger diameter if your hair is more than six inches below the shoulder or if you want big, wavy curls), a holding product (mousse or blow-dry setting spray works well), some small clips, and a nonaerosol, light-hold mist.

2. On wet hair, apply the holding product at the roots, using your hands and fingers to work it through to the end of the hair shaft. Most of the product should be at the roots, but distribute a little toward the tips where it functions as a

Diffusing the Diffuser

A diffuser is a great tool for encouraging curl. It is a simple $20 attachment you can clip onto your blow-dryer. In simple terms, the air of a blow-dryer can blow your curly hair around too much and disturb your curl formation. That's why, if you're looking to control your natural curl, the wet-set technique is better than using a blow-dryer.

But if you want faster drying, you can use your blow-dryer with a diffuser. The diffuser takes away all the air of a blow-dryer but keeps all the heat; it dries curly hair without blowing on it, using the heat to lock the curl in place. If you have some curl and want to accentuate this look, a diffuser is definitely a great way to go.

Successful results depend on the right technique. Follow the instructions in the Controlled Curls section (page 113) up to and including step 7. Now, instead of squeezing your hair every fifteen minutes, simply attach and use your diffuser. Try to get to your roots first because ends are finer hair strands, drying much faster as a consequence. If you dry the ends first and then try to get at your roots, you end up overdrying your ends. Hang your head over, letting your hair fall downward to the floor, and place the diffuser as close to the roots as possible, remembering to gently rotate around your head. Never hold your diffuser still. This gives too much heat in one place. Rotate and move, up and down, left and right.

All you have to do now is follow steps 9, 10, and 11 of the Controlled Curls section and enjoy your bountiful and beautiful curly hair.

Curling Irons

Curling irons are a great contemporary quick-fix tool for at-home hairstyling, especially effective for creating curl and movement in straight hair. Indeed, you can substitute a curling iron for both the dryer and the round brush and employ almost the exact same technique with the same result—only it's quicker and easier.

Of course there is a downside. Placing direct heat from an iron on your hair has the potential to create curls that appear a little too formed, a little too perfect. It can also fry your hair. The big rule: Don't hold the iron on your hair too long. At best, this damages your daily curls; at worst, it burns your hair bone-dry. The fix: Buy an iron with a thermometer control tool and place your iron on medium heat rather than high heat.

In addition to abandoning your dryer and brush, the other big change when using an iron is that you use a different product. Instead of a bodybuilding product, you need a thermal protector. Apply it as you would your bodybuilder (outlined in step 2 of "Creating Curl," page 114) and follow the remaining techniques. Remember, if you take small sections, you create tight little ringlets, while bigger sections create softer, looser waves.

The time you leave your hair curled on the iron is determined by when you can feel heat on your hair. Once you can feel heat on the section wrapped around the curling iron, it's time to take it out. Now you can just ruffle your roots to unravel the curl as desired. Looking for a firmer curl and are worried it might fall away? Once you've taken out the iron, use a small clip to fasten the curl into place at its base, wait for it to cool totally, and now gently run your fingers through your curls. This definitely gives you your strongest curl. If it ends up too strong, first brush it out; if it's still too firm, use the heat of the dryer to break the wave a little.

The thermal protector prevents your hair from drying out while still providing the base and preparation you need. But please note: No thermal protector, or any other product or tool, can protect hair that is already dry and damaged. If this is you, page 167 provides the answers you need.

I also recommend that you invest in a high-quality moisturizing conditioner if you are using any sort of iron regularly. This improves the condition of your hair by replacing the inevitable loss of moisture caused by the heat of the curling iron. Here are a couple of other things to remember, if you choose a curling iron instead of a blow-dryer and brush. You can buy a good ceramic curling iron for around $40. Irons come in different shapes and sizes; smaller-diameter barrels (1") create tight curls; bigger-diameter barrels (2"–3") create bigger, softer curls or waves. A medium-sized barrel (1½"–2") suffices for most people's needs, especially the creating curl technique just showcased.

great setting aid to help hold curls in place all day.

3. Use your hair dryer to power-dry 80 percent of the moisture out of your hair. Don't worry about particular sections; instead, make sure it's evenly 70 percent or 80 percent dry all over.

4. Now attach the hair dryer's nozzle. Start wrapping sections of hair around the round brush. It doesn't matter if you start at the front or the back; you're going to be going all over anyway. But remember, the sections on top and on the sides are much easier to get at than those in the back, so when you're learning the technique, perhaps practice on top first while you get the hang of it. In any case,

wrap a piece of hair around the round brush in a section no bigger than the size of the barrel. Then hold the dryer six to ten inches from the section and power-dry all the moisture away. You can finish with a cold shot of air to further set the curl. In effect, this method works exactly the same way the old-fashioned rollers created curl for your mom.

5. Once done, unravel the brush (never pull it out), allowing the curl to set in place. Then, with your hands, rewind the curled section into a barrel and lock it into place with a small clip.

6. Repeat this process in sections all over your head. It's more important to place the curls around the front, top, and sides, but try to get some nice curls going at the back, too. Supersexy curls draped across the back really help to complete the look. With a little practice it should take no longer than twenty minutes to do your whole head.

7. When you've prepared each section, lightly mist all over your hair with nonaerosol holding spray and allow to totally cool—approximately ten minutes.

8. Now unclip your sections, unravel, and finger-style. It's much better to finger-style at this phase because the power of a brush will break the curl you've worked to create, whereas your fingers will aid a soft

and tousled finish. Gently rake your fingers through to the roots and then loosely shake out your hair.

9. If the look is too curly, you can use the heat of the dryer to break the wave a little. Just lightly blowing in some heat to your curls loosens their formation.

10. If you're in a rush, or are struggling with the technique, you can replace your dryer and brush with a curling iron. This is easier and quicker, and simplifies the difficult task of styling the back sections. On the downside, a curling iron creates a stronger curl, so it may appear false or forced.

Time to Updo

Now that we've covered the basics, it should be much easier to make your hair work for you. Remember, styling should be creative and fun. If you can grasp and apply these techniques, you're ready to play with some more complicated styles and even updos—great for looking more individual, more polished. And who doesn't want that?

PONYTAIL

Styling hair into a sleek and sophisticated ponytail is the best place to start your updo

education. It's a great way to vary your look, and best of all, it's a supersimple, easy-to-do technique.

1. To wear a ponytail, you need length to your shoulders at least.

2. I recommend a covered elastic band or, better, a bungee band. These have hooks on either side that are great for holding your ponytail in place. If you've never seen a bungee, check the glossary at the back of this book for a full description, or simply ask in your local beauty supply store.

3. The key to a successful pony is in the preparation. It's not totally necessary to wash your hair beforehand. In fact, slightly dirty hair can even be better because the hair is a little rougher, which in turn helps your pins and grips do what they need to do: hold tight. If you are going to wash and blow-dry your hair beforehand, you need to create some texture for the hooks to grip. To do this, simply apply a preparation product (mousse, foam, or thickening spray) and execute the basic blow-dry highlighted at the start of this chapter. So long as you don't brush your hair smooth at the end, this creates ample texture for your ponytail.

4. Now that your hair is properly prepared for a ponytail, use your hands or a brush to gather your hair into a high or low ponytail as desired. Now pull on your band or cord and hook and wrap it around the base, nice and tight. When you run out of cord, simply hook the cord into the base of your pony to complete your ponytail.

5. Whenever you create a ponytail, the tightness at the nape can make or break the look. This area has looser skin; therefore, it's important to keep your head upright when forming your ponytail. If your head is forward or tucked down when you secure, as soon as you lift your head this area becomes baggy, loose, and amateurish. A simple precaution: Hold your chin up.

6. A low ponytail is a more casual, free-and-easy daytime look; it should sit below the nape of your neck. A high ponytail is definitely more of a nighttime look. It gives you lots of lift and lots of drama, and emphasizes your cheekbones, making you look polished and refined.

FRENCH TWIST

A great alternative to the ponytail is the French twist. The twist is trickier than a ponytail—it's a salon-professional technique, after all—but with practice I'm confident it will become a fantastic addition to your own hairstyling.

1. You need bobby pins, big hairpins, hair spray, and a flat brush. It's better to leave your hair unwashed for this

technique, as one or two days of unwashed hair give your hair a natural texture that works better for holding your twist in place. If you need to wash your hair, no problem. Just make sure to blow-dry in some product (a holding spray works fine) to create the texture you need.

2. Rather than pulling your hair into one big piece as you would with a ponytail, you create a seam—a lovely folded pattern—across the back of your head. To do this, the left and right sides of your hair must be brushed back. I recommend making the part on one side—that's much sexier than splitting your hairline, and face, down the middle. So to begin, use the flat brush to make a nice side part and brush each side of your hair through to the back.

Remember to keep your chin up, which ensures that your twist is tight; if you let your chin fall, the skin at the nape of your neck is loose and so is your twist.

3. Now that your hair is brushed back, you can fold and twist one side of the seam into place. It's best first to work on the side near the part and use your hands to cup the seam nice and tight. This is simpler than it sounds. Just take your brushed-back section, spray it with a little holding spray, and gather it into your hand—almost as if you're gathering it into a low ponytail—and twist and hold this piece of hair in place over the back of the center of your head. Make sure to gather in all excess hair. If at the end you want to loosely drape a few pieces out, that's fine, but for now focus on getting all the brushed-back hair into your twist.

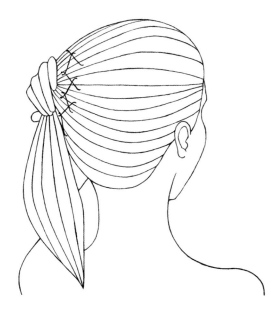

4. Next, place three bobby pins in the bottom, middle, and top of your half a twist, the half a seam you've just created, pinning it back and flat. Start at the bottom because this helps support your seam structure. Lock the pins inside your seam, weaving one into another if possible. These bobby pins keep it nice and sleek, but you should now also use a little more hair spray on the side of the seam to further aid hold and sleekness.

5. You're in great shape. You have your base—one side of the twist—held back with bobby pins, across the center of your head. This means that one half of the preparation is firmly in place. Now take the other side, the half with most of the hair, brushed back in the same manner, but also make sure to brush the hair over the pins of the half a seam you've just created. Grab this second section with your hand, low and central to the back of your head, then twist your hair upward, over the top of your original seam, and cup it in place with your hands. You are cupping the area where you placed your three original bobby pins.

6. Take one big hairpin and place it where your fingertips are applying pressure to hold the second part of your twist in place. It's also important to place the pin in from the same direction your hair has been brushed back. For example, if you're coming from the left, place the pin in from that direction, too. This aids the stability of your twist. Be sure to catch the top surface of the original folded twist with your pin, and once the pin goes in, sharply twist the pin back, fixing it back on itself in an action much akin to a classic sewing technique—back and forth, over and under.

7. Now spritz again with your hair spray to set and sleek the second part of your perfect twist.

8. Don't worry. Done right, the pressure of the pin going back and the tension of the fold easily hold up the heaviest of hair.

Pin Basics

Three pins are critical for the success of any updo:

- Regular hairpins are ideal for holding a large amount of hair.

- Fine hairpins are perfect for the detailing of any updo because they disappear into your hair.

- Bobby pins, a combination of smooth edges and grooves that hold together to grip firmly in place, are a must. They are easy to use and especially effective at holding back unruly hair.

Two Common Problems

There are a couple of common problems that I hear clients talk about every day. These little niggles infuriate clients because they appear so simple and so silly, and yet they have the potential to destroy your carefully constructed styling.

Flyaways are unavoidable for anyone who blow-dries her hair. We all lose hairs every day, and they replenish themselves every day, too. The problem is that those lovely new hairs are shorter and fail to make it around the brush when you blow-dry. Instead, infuriatingly, they stand up on end and can cause your new polished do to flop. The solution: hair spray. After styling, simply spritz a strong-hold hair spray on any flyaways to flatten them out. Problem solved.

Split Ends occur on the tips, the oldest part of each hair strand. Normally, between seven and ten weeks after your last cut, those poor old ends start to fray, becoming thin, weak, and brittle, before finally splitting apart for good. We all love long hair, but let's be realistic: Split ends do not look good. A good defrizz serum and a well-executed smooth blow out help to reduce the *appearance* of split ends and, as a consequence of the split ends, frizz. (It won't make them disappear totally, and as the day wears on they become more and more noticeable.) But there's no product or styling technique I know of after twenty-five years in the industry to get rid of split ends other than a cut.

Take the hit, deal with the problem immediately, and regrow your hair to be healthy and sexy.

Summing It All Up

This chapter is the heart of this book—it's the chapter you should use the most. Keep this book by your vanity mirror and create salon-perfect hair every day. These are the techniques that I employ, and if they work for me, they will work for you.

I've given you a thorough explanation of which products and tools do which jobs. This is important, because applying the right products and tools for the look you want is more than half of the styling-at-home battle. By using my guidelines on products and brushes and my tips on curling irons and straightening irons, you always have the tools to get the job you want done, done right.

Everyone should learn the basic blow-dry. If you know how to do this, you need make only slight variations in your technique and the necessary adjustments to your products and styling tools to create lots of different looks. Remember, whether your hair is long or short, straight or curly, whether you want to boost up your volume or smooth out your kinks, or whether you want to control or create curls, this chapter has the technique for you.

Master the techniques for styling at home and you'll find many ways that you can manipulate your hair for a variety of fabulous, fashion-forward styles.

6. Great Hair Color

A great hairstyle becomes even better when it's complemented by great color.

If you want to look more polished, more pulled together, more modern, great hair color will do that for you. It is also an opportunity to brighten up your best features. Hair color tends to draw more attention to your face, especially the eyes. Color creates more magic.

For me, this is a fascinating and artistic area of a hairdresser's work, because with color, a stylist can add vibrancy, texture, depth, and contrast. With modern hair color technology improving by leaps and bounds, today's woman has a rich and varied selection from which she can choose the perfect hue to change and revitalize her look. Today, hair color mirrors the ever-evolving fashion and cosmetic trends; dynamic, face-fitting, and youthful color work is part and parcel of the style savvy because it epitomizes a luxurious look. When your hair becomes dehydrated and dull, color gives you back that vivacious glow.

What's more, color deals with our emotions. Often when we see color, it affects our feelings. It's not just a coincidence that red can be associated with hot, blue with cold, green with envy, yellow with cowardice. How do you feel when you wear a bright and colorful outfit, as opposed to a dark and somber one? It's the same thing with hair. Blondes are said to have more fun; redheads are thought to be a fiery

breed; and brunettes are known as earthy, natural, and cheerful.

Color gives you the chance to change and personalize your identity. Just look at what Blond Ambition did for Madonna, what hot red tones did for *Pretty Woman* Julia Roberts, and what the timeless elegance of Audrey Hepburn's brunette locks did to make her, to this day, a fashion goddess.

It's not just the movie stars. Every day in my salon I see the power of the color transformation. One that sticks in my mind is a longtime client, Lisa, who was a virgin head. Not her term—mine. It's a stylist's phrase for a woman

For me, this is a fascinating and artistic area of a hairdresser's work, because with color, a stylist can add vibrancy, texture, depth, and contrast.

who has never colored her hair. Lisa was nervous. In her midthirties, with dark brown hair that had a rich natural glow, she was distressed that she was starting to go gray. At first the gray was only underneath and it was no big deal if a stray strand popped through. But then it started coming through more and more. She had two kids but wasn't ready to be such an out-of-date mom.

At the same time she knew she was losing that rich natural glow and was starting to feel like she was losing part of her identity, too. Lisa wanted back that dimension and shine, although she was worried that applied hair color would never match her natural hue. I told her that would not be the case.

First, I explained her options for coloring the gray. If she wanted to maintain as much of her natural color as possible, we would paint over the gray with highlights to cover it. The upkeep wouldn't be crazy—coming in every eight to twelve weeks just to add extra gloss and shine and cover the roots.

If she wanted to be a little adventurous, she could color the gray by playing with her allover shade. A classic virgin head, Lisa opted for as little change as possible. The highlights covered her gray perfectly and she looked just like herself.

Then one day, she plunked herself down in my chair and announced, "I like my cut. That's not changing, but I'm bored. What can I do to change it up?"

"Color," I replied. "Go a tone or two lighter so it's not too drastic. It'll cover the gray and give you a brilliant boost of shine."

"Let's go for it," she said.

And we did.

Five years later, she's a dedicated color client. A little darker and more mysterious in the winter, a little brighter with subtle hints of light brown and blond in the summer. She always

remembers her first time and she always comments on how the darker shades make her feel like a modern mom who's ready for fall, while the lighter shades make her feel young, and fresh, and new, just in time for spring.

Color has a wide range of worthy purposes: enhancing an existing hair color with richness and glow; creating a unique statement of self-expression; adding face-framing shape, or highlighting the shape of a particular haircut; revitalizing dry, dull, faded-out hair color; covering, blending, or masking gray. But more than anything, if you already have a great cut, and you're using this book to better style your hair every day, then get into great color to promote even more youthfulness and beauty with the shiny personal definition color can provide.

If you've never had color before, or if a fully fledged color regimen already features in your style locker, this chapter will give you a better understanding of the process so you can make hair color succeed for you. I show you how hair color works; what the different salon service options can do for you; how you can use the level system, lifestyle, personality, and current trends to help pick the right color for you; the best approach for your consultation; ideas for blondes, brunettes, redheads, and grays; the aftercare process; and tackling at-home hair color.

The Level System

Throughout this book, I've talked about how to work with your natural features and your natural beauty to create easy-to-achieve looks that also give you that Wow! factor. The same principle applies to color. If you work within the natural parameters of what your hair can most easily handle, getting a positive change and a successful color are pretty straightforward, while the upkeep and maintenance are trouble-free. For a more dramatic change, you can go out of your comfort zone, but then there's a higher risk of the color causing damage or being an unsuitable tone for you, and you definitely need to dedicate more time to the aftercare process.

The easiest way to assess your own natural parameters of how far you can change your hair color, and what you may need to do to push the limits of those parameters, is the level system, which values the lightness or darkness of hair color:

1. Black
2. Very dark brown
3. Dark brown
4. Medium brown
5. Light brown
6. Dark blond
7. Medium blond
8. Light blond
9. Very light blond
10. Lightest blond

(Redheads, I know you feel left out of this, but don't you worry—I cover the glorious shade of red later.)

Common practice in color dictates that for guaranteed hair health and integrity, you should stay within three to four levels of your natural hair color. The reason: If you go beyond the three to four-level safety net (and most people who do, want to go blonder), the chemicals needed to change the hair color so radically are much, much stronger. This strong chemical process is generally called bleaching, and at best it leaves your hair dry, porous, and in need of dedicated aftercare to keep up the color; at worst, it can literally leave your hair broken in two (although that generally happens on fragile or previously overprocessed hair). A good colorist would not perform the service if he or she thought there was a high risk of this happening. Plus, the more levels you change, the more the roots show, and the more often you'll have to touch them up.

So if you are a very dark brown (level 2), for instance, medium to light brown is the biggest natural change you should undertake. On the other hand, if you're a natural light brown (level 5), you can go to light blond or, if you want to go darker, very dark brown. However, it's important to note that this system is based on your natural hair color. For example, if you want to go from your natural hue, say black (level 1) to lightest blond (level 10), you *cannot* make a three-level change to medium brown and then another three-level change to medium blond and then another three-level change to lightest blond, thinking this is a safer bet than a bleaching process. It doesn't work like that. Your natural canvas is your natural hair color and will always be considered your base, natural level. If you

> ## Many people look sensational with a dramatic change, especially if they can find a tone that suits their complexion.

want to go further, the bleaching process will take you there.

My goal is to make your great hair color easy and fun and natural, so I strongly promote staying within these levels of color change, because this comfort zone offers guaranteed healthy hair, less aftercare, and a more relaxed color service (because you won't be in the chair worrying about how much damage it's going to cause). You'll get a phenomenal, fashion-forward change to the way you look, and you can still go lighter whenever you want to, just not more than three to four levels lighter.

The other big reason for staying within the recommended levels of your natural color is that this guarantees that your new hair color complements your complexion. Go beyond these levels and there's a chance your hair color, having changed so dramatically, will make you look washed-out or too stark, depending on whether you've gone lighter or darker. If you are

dead set on going for more than the recommended levels of change, make sure your hair is in good condition first, be prepared for the aftercare, and then go for it. Many people look sensational with a dramatic change, especially if they can find a tone that suits their complexion.

Finally, as I briefly mentioned earlier, reds do not appear in the level system. This is because less than 2 percent of the population is naturally red. For you, your colorist will establish the depth of your redness and recommend colors accordingly. However, red is deemed a fairly light hair color, so depending on the depth of your red, you can usually find a level anywhere between light brown and light blond.

Pigment and Porosity

When it comes to coloring, there are two other things you should know about: pigment and porosity. Each person has either more natural red pigment or more natural yellow pigment. More red makes for darker natural hair color; more yellow makes for lighter natural color. This is especially important for red pigment people because if you make your dark hair light by chemical bleaching, you can be left with a brassy blond, particularly a few weeks in, when

the tone starts to fade. Because chemical bleaching strips out your natural hair color, it exposes the pigment in your hair—red. After the natural color has been stripped away, a colorist tones the hair into the shade you've asked for, normally very successfully, but as the shade starts to fade, or if the application was not successful, you're left with that brassiness you may have already noticed on some bleach blondes. Now you know why bleaching is, to a certain extent, a risky color service—exposing your natural red pigment can cause brassiness. This is also why I recommend ash tones for bleach blondes. Ash colors are the best at neutralizing the brassy effect.

Porous hair is dry and dehydrated, often with split ends. If your hair has high porosity, it will react inconsistently to hair color. When you apply color, the cuticle (outer) layer opens up to take in the color and then closes shut fairly rapidly. But if the hair is porous, the cuticle remains open and you get less consistent color results. Most likely the color at the root—where the hair is always most healthy—will take well and will be shiny and new, whereas near the ends it won't be nearly as bright. Porous hair is most common on those who have colored their hair a lot (that's why we always see the best results on virgin heads) without taking the necessary aftercare, and also those who use lots of heat and hot tools, without taking the proper precautions. If your hair becomes porous and dry, it is better to improve the health before going for a new color service. Use deep conditioning treatments and keratin-based hair strengtheners to get the health back.

Color Tones

The other major factor in choosing a hair color is tone. Let's say that you're a natural level 5, light brown, and you've decided to move three levels lighter into a light blond. Now you can start to think about what tone of light blond you'd like to be. Tone refers to whether a color is warm or cool. The warm colors are tones that are created in the red, orange, and yellow range; the cool colors are tones that are created in the blue, green, and violet range. If you're looking for a light blond and you want a warm tone, then strawberry blond is a typical color tone for you. On the other hand, if you want to be light blond with a cool tone, then a whitish ash blond is a more typical color tone. Or say you've decided to go from dark brown to light brown. You can choose a warm tone like ruby red or chestnut, or you can choose a cool tone like frosty brown or caramel.

Ways to Color

I'll talk more about all the hair color shades, features, and benefits as I move forward, but the next step is to know and understand the variety of hair color options. There are different types of hair color, and they involve putting different kinds and different strengths of ingredients and chemicals into your hair in order to create the color change you desire. Each one has different capabilities: Some change your hair color minimally, some change your hair color radically, and others are right in the middle. They also all have different levels of harshness and last a different amount of time. The stronger the chemical process, the more potential to change radically, the harsher it is on your hair (don't be put off by this; yes, chemical color can be a touch harsh on the hair, but it's normally not too serious and can be easily counterbalanced with the right aftercare), and the longer-lasting the

color is. It's important to know what you're getting into, so let's take a look at the different types of hair color.

Semipermanent is a temporary hair color lasting a maximum of twelve shampoos. It is a vegetable-based color rinse that provides a light color coating that "stains" the outside portion of the hair rather than penetrating into the hair shaft for longer-lasting, more vivid color, which is what chemical demipermanent and permanent color processes do. The best features of semipermanent color are that it is damage- and risk-free, and it adds shine, fullness, and depth in a variety of subtle tones. When semipermanent color is applied to light brown to black hair, you generally get a warm red glow to your hue, while lighter blond shades tend to display hints of gold-red.

Semipermanent also has big limitations. It doesn't lighten hair color, it's not very effective if you want to blend out gray, and it is unsuitable for previously bleached or highlighted hair. Over-all, however, it is a great way to try hair color for the first time—you can experiment without the risk, and there is no maintenance of the new growth (because the color fades out before the roots have a chance to show). Just know that you won't see a big, dramatic change, and the quality never equals a demipermanent or permanent color. Instead, work with your colorist to use this process to shift the tone of your color for the better, depositing extra shine and luster. One final note: Semipermanent color, being such a light, gentle, and limited color service, is not offered by all salons, so check with the salon first.

Demipermanent (also known as "deposit only" as a reference to the way it works), color contains low levels of peroxide in a chemical formula that does penetrate (as opposed to semipermanent, which just adds that color stain) into the hair shaft for long-lasting and vivid hair color. Because it is a gentle chemical process, it does not lighten your hair color at all, but it is ideal for blending low to medium levels of gray to look less gray while adding more luster and depth, for freshening up faded permanent colors, and for depositing changes in tone—most commonly, and most effectively, in the gold, red, copper, or burgundy range. It can also correct previously "gone wrong" color and is used for lowlighting (the opposite of highlighting, it adds lowlights that are darker than your natural tone for depth and subtlety). Demipermanent is great if you don't want to lighten your hair overall; it's a mild, risk- and commitment-free process that adds real shine and gloss. Typically it lasts around six weeks.

Permanent color can add an infinite array of depth and tone to your color for your widest range of choices. It is by far the best option for mid- to high levels of gray and, apart from bleaching, is the only way to take your hair color lighter. But with this type of color, three to four levels lighter is definitely the most you can go, whereas bleach lightens your hair a lot more. Like demipermanent, permanent color uses a chemical peroxide process that locks color into the hair shaft, but by using higher levels of the chemical it provides stronger, more dynamic color, offering a complete range of tones. That's the biggest benefit: the ability to go light or dark in a variety of modern color tones. For gray hair, permanent color provides complete natural-looking coverage, even if you're 100 percent salt and pepper. Single-process permanent color stays strong and bright for around six weeks. There is a commitment here, because you need to use color-safe shampoos and conditioners, and the occasional deep-conditioning treatment will also help you keep the integrity in the color of your hair. However, damage to the hair is minimal. Making sure you and your colorist choose a palette that suits you—and that you're happy with—should be your biggest focus.

Hair lighteners (a salon-friendly way of saying "bleach") are necessary to lighten more than three to four levels. This is a strong chemical bleaching process. It changes hair from dark to light, performs strong highlighting, and can create pastel blond hues. It works by taking out your natural hair color and then replacing it with a new, much lighter tone—

that's why in the salon it's commonly referred to as the bleach and tone.

This is a high commitment because the regrowth needs retouching every four to six weeks; otherwise you have dark roots with blond hair, which is neither a youthful nor an attractive way to go. Another factor to consider is that your hair inevitably suffers some damage. It'll certainly be more dry and brittle than normal, and more prone to frizz. You'll also have to be careful with heat tools like blow-dryers and hot irons because the mild heat-induced damage these tools themselves can cause only accentuates any dryness and brittleness in your hair.

Salon Services

Now you are ready to get down to the salon and explore some of these exciting color options for yourself. The modern hair salon offers a range of great services that are based around the four basic hair color processes (semipermanent, demipermanent, permanent, and bleaching) and provides a whole host of different options for you. Let's take a look.

HIGHLIGHTS

Highlights give you shimmering variation in tone that adds depth and dimension. They give you more sparkle and more gloss. They are also a good way to blend small patches of gray. Your colorist will weave intricately through small

sections of your hair, sealing them in foils or packets and giving them a lighter color. Highlighting comes in a variety of guises, and knowing them all will help you chose the right type for you.

Face-framing highlights are a great way to start any highlighting journey because they always look sensational. Highlights are placed from ear to ear, perfectly framing the shape of your haircut and emphasizing the features of your face, especially your eyes. To keep it up, you need a redo every eight to twelve weeks.

Half-head highlights focus on the top and the sides of your head. They provide nice definition to the central part of any haircut, adding tone and shine where you want it most. To keep it up, you need a redo every eight to twelve weeks. This is a great service if you've already had a full head of highlights and are going back to the salon for a redo two or three months down the line, because the colorist now focuses the color application at the roots, where it's needed most. This saves you the extra cash you might otherwise spend on another full head of highlights.

Full-head highlights give you ripples of color everywhere. This is probably the most popular in-salon color service—the dynamic, allover gloss and sheen never fail to leave clients thrilled. To keep it up, you need a redo every eight to twelve weeks.

Lowlights are just like highlighting, with the same range of options (face-framing through full-head lowlights, as well as partial foils), but instead of lifting the color to a lighter tone, it adds in color that is a shade or two darker than your natural level. This creates real depth, dimension, and the illusion of thickness to any haircut. It also brings balance to hair that has been colored too light in the past.

Foils and packets are used for any type of the above-mentioned highlighting. The foils are woven through your hair in chunky sections or in much finer, slim sections. This is important because chunkier foils give you a more definitive, heavier finish; a finer foil placement creates a more natural, lighter feel. One quick note for naturally curly hair: I recommend a thicker, chunkier, heavier finish highlight. This is better for you because fine highlights get lost in the curl while thicker ones are more prominent.

Partial foil is generally done as a touch-up for previous highlighting or lowlighting. Instead of paying for another full-highlight service, you can get a partial foil just to touch up the

Highlights give you shimmering variation in tone that adds depth and dimension. They give you more sparkle and more gloss.

regrowth. (The regrowth is the roots that have grown in in your natural color.) This is a great way to refresh and revitalize your highlights and can be done any time you feel it's necessary.

Slicing goes beyond the thicker, chunkier highlights you can get with foils. The principle is the same, but rather than weaving through the hair in ultrafine sections, we take a full panel of hair and color it all. This makes a much bigger impact than a high- or lowlight; it's a bolder, stronger color statement. It's hip and cool, but make sure it's going to work for you. Touch-ups are required at eight- to ten-week intervals.

Single process covers all of your hair with one new color. For example, if you're a natural light brown, you may go for a single process that makes you dark blond all over (if you want your whole hair color to be lighter) or you may go for a single process that makes you dark brown all over (if you want your whole hair color to be darker). This is a great way to revitalize yourself with a beautiful color-enhanced, brand-new you. Just make sure to choose a color you love, and that suits you, your personality, and complexion. Single process is also the right choice when you want to mask the gray in hair that has become more than 50 percent salt and pepper. For an even stronger change, a single process can easily be combined with a highlight (in the salon this is typically called a single process with a highlight or, for more brevity, a double process). You need to get single-process color redone every six weeks.

Bleach and tone is for those who have decided to go very blond all over. Your hair is bleached to take out the natural color pigment and then toned to the appropriate shade. Going blond is a dramatic change that can make you feel sensational, like an entirely new person. Just be sure blond is going to work for you and commit to the aftercare process. Repeat applications are required every four to six weeks to cover your roots and refresh the overall blondness.

Glaze is a new salon-friendly way of saying tone. It puts a new tone into your hair color, enhancing the sharpness, shine, and definition. Though it's usually the finishing touch (adding the final tonal elements to the color) to the other salon hair color services, you can ask for a glaze appointment, which is a cheap and quick way to add a bit more luster into your hair color.

Corrective color is the remedy when hair color goes wrong. A bad at-home hair color or an overly ambitious salon procedure can lead to the need for color correction. Most commonly, corrective color uses chemical agents that break down the color molecules, making them fade

Lifestyle and Personality

Choose color to match your personality and lifestyle, which means taking into consideration not only the shade but also the level of commitment to color that you're willing to make. Think about this carefully, because once you enlist in a full-color regimen—a demipermanent, permanent, or bleaching process—the only true way to get out of it is to cut out the color in your hair. Literally, this means letting your hair grow and cutting off *all* the hair that has been previously colored. Why? Because if you don't recolor colored hair, you end up with a line of demarcation. Your natural hair color starts to grow back in and contrasts badly with your chemically altered hair color, leaving you looking messy and unkempt. The only way to cover up the regrowth is by touching up your roots. You don't always have to do this with permanent color on top of permanent color—touch-ups can be done with a demipermanent process—but, either way, you become locked into a color regimen. So if you are considering a color, especially if you are getting into it for the first time, think first about what level of commitment you are willing to make. If you don't want a big commitment and want to keep your color easy to care for, go for a color that is close to your natural tone or for a semipermanent color that fades away gradually. If you want more change or more permanent color, you have to be prepared to keep it up.

On the bright side, changing your hair color can really enhance the way you look, and it might even change your personality. Color has great potential to change how you feel about yourself. Just ask the girl who goes platinum blond. She immediately *feels* blond, girly, and flirty with Marilyn Monroe–inspired confidence. It's not only blondness that has this effect. Go dark, go light, go red—any of these popular color palettes can totally change the way you look and feel. You can even create an alter ego for yourself. Color is something you can have a lot of fun with.

away more quickly. However, it often takes repeat corrective processes to remove the unwanted color, so be sure to speak with your colorist about the time frame and the cost. This is the most difficult color service to execute because simply putting another color on top of a bad color doesn't work. The colorist needs to slowly, surely, and carefully take out the bad hair color, and this can take repeat trips to the salon over an extended period of time. Before you start down this road, a thorough consultation is essential.

The Aging Process

As women age and gray starts to creep into their hair, their skin tone naturally changes as well. As we get older, our skin color becomes paler and it has more opacity. This means that if you're in your forties or fifties and you're still coloring your hair the same shade as when you were younger, it may well be that your skin tone and

hair color no longer complement each other. This is very common and often results in older ladies, who have colored their hair dark for years, looking very pale. If your skin tone has developed more opacity over the years, then you should be looking for a lighter hair color because changes in your hair and skin colors are intrinsically linked. Don't be afraid to adapt. We're all aging, it's natural, and the trick is to stay one step ahead. Get great hair color on top of a great cut with the right styling, and you can easily look ten years younger.

Generally speaking, if your gray covers 25 percent or less of your hair, then some subtle highlights are enough to cover the gray areas. If you're in the 25 percent to 50 percent gray range, you need an allover demipermanent, single-process hair color to take the gray away. If you're more than 50 percent gray, go for a permanent, single-process to mask the gray completely.

Common Hair Hues

If you're ready to try a new color, here are some things for you to consider about all the common hair hues.

BLONDES AND BLEACH BLONDES

Not everyone has to bleach and tone her hair to go blond. Normally, hair that was naturally blond in childhood and has darkened to mousy brown as time has gone by is the perfect natural base to go blond without bleaching. Not only is the hair more suitable (because the natural color will be much closer to natural blond), but it's also likely that your skin tone and eye color are a great match for blondness. If you're naturally darker and you go bleach blond, the texture of your hair will change, becoming slightly thicker because of the strong chemical process, as well as dry, possibly brittle, and more prone to frizz. If your hair has a lot of hair color history and is not in the best condition to begin with, then breakage of the hair shaft is a real possibility. You are lifting out all of your natural hair color and then depositing a completely new tone, so prepare for a high commitment to the right aftercare. My favorite blond tones include cool Nordic blonde, warm strawberry, and bold gold blond. A dynamic tone like one of these can turn you into a blistering-hot blonde. One more word on this: Bleaching tends to get better results on naturally smoother, straighter hair types. On curly or wavy

hair, more often than not, the look fails, and I usually advise against it.

Finally, there is a recent technical innovation: high-lift blonds. This is the newest way to make your hair color lighter, and pushes the boundaries. As I've mentioned, if you want to shift your hair color more than three to four levels lighter, then bleaching is your number one option. However, high-lift blondes are able to shift hair color four to five levels lighter without the need for a chemical bleaching process. This is a great innovation and generally works well, though it is still a strong process and has an effect on the overall health of your hair, but not nearly as much as a bleach and tone. For my money, I still recommend staying within three levels for a good hair-health safety net, but this is definitely an option worth considering if you're looking for extra levels of lightness in your hair.

BRUNETTES

It's great to be a brunette because brown hair always seems to look thick and glossy, healthy and happy. Not only that, but natural brunettes can use almost all color tones with excellent results. In my experience, brunettes get their best results by going a shade or two lighter than their natural color. It just seems to add an extra dab of warmth, richness, and luster. Great options are caramels, chestnuts, and light coffee browns, which all add depth, shimmer, and shine, making you a truly beautiful brunette. Perhaps the only big challenge is if you want to go allover bleach blond. I've already talked

about the damage this can cause, but in addition, intensely light shades on brown hair can look very much out of place, even a bit grimy, because often the skin tone doesn't have the right contrast for a much lighter hair color. However, highlights are a great way to put ribbons of blondness into your hair without the commitment of a single process. Go for soft blond or light gold highlights—both provide a glittering contrast to your natural brown hue.

RAMPED-UP REDS

I love red hair because it is so striking. When I see a great color-enhanced red, it immediately grabs my attention for its uniqueness and

individuality. You see blondes and brunettes everywhere, but red is such a distinctive color that it immediately defines the personality of that person. And reds offer you lots of variety with tones in the orange, violet, and blond ranges, which gives you loads of scope to be creative and get a one-of-a-kind, individual look.

If you're interested in going red, I recommend a single process to give you strong, head-turning color. However, if you are curious about red but aren't ready for the full commitment, start with some subtle high- or lowlighting. For darker brunettes, a red highlight adds richness and dimension. For more mid- to light browns, I recommend dark red lowlights for depth and subtlety. For blondes, red highlights present more of a challenge, as getting the colors to contrast correctly is tougher, but well-executed soft, strawberry-red highlights look great.

For a full single process, try deep dark reds with hints of violet. My other favorite shades include ruby red, burgundy red, cherry red, crimson, and scarlet. All are great tones sure to make you feel special and unique. Remember, red tones work best with fair or tan skin. If you have a pearly red skin tone, work with your colorist to find a hair tone that matches the shade of your skin. Think about eye color, too: If you have green, blue, or gray eyes, reds really make your eyes pop for a sensational color-coordinated do.

The only downside with red is that it's the fastest color to fade. The red color pigments tend to wash away much more quickly because the actual red color molecules are smaller

> You see blondes and brunettes everywhere, but red is such a distinctive color that it immediately defines the personality of that person.

than any others and can escape more easily, especially with overexposure to the sun. That makes aftercare critical, with a good color-safe red-tint shampoo and conditioner as your go-to products.

TREND CONSCIOUS

Color trends come quickly. It's great to stay contemporary, but don't chase all the color trends—they won't all work for you. For example, it's hot to be blond, but not if you're a brunette!

There also are trends in the type of color work stylists do. It may be a time of more multiple layering of color, of strong blocks of color, or of very subtle high- or lowlighting. The color manufacturers play a big part in this as well. As technology improves, the manufacturers produce more and more dynamic color. Maybe this year they're introducing cool frosty browns or ashy blond tones that everyone wants to try. This may very well influence what color your colorist recommends for you.

Spot color trends on the runways, in magazines, in beauty columns, and on celebrities. Even better, ask your colorist to keep you current with the latest trends. But most important, choose a color and a trend that suit you and your own individual style. To simplify this task, sort color trends into two distinct seasons: spring/summer and fall/winter. As your basic rule of thumb, go lighter in the summer for beautiful, bright color and darker in winter for more depth and dimension. This also suits the elements and our skin tones because lighter tones definitely glow more on brighter days, and darker, more dimensional tones suit the more gloomy winter months. Overall, spring is your best time to change. It's a natural time of renewal, giving you the chance to revamp your color, all for the better.

The Consultation

Just as with a cut, a color appointment begins with a consultation. And remember, if you're still trying to decide what hair color direction you want to go in, and/or it's your first visit to a particular colorist, you can set up a consultation before booking your appointment. The consultation lets you get to know your colorist and find out what he or she recommends for you. Just like with a haircut, bringing pictures is a massive help to you and your colorist. One note of caution: Don't expect your hair color to be an exact match of the color in the picture. How hair color turns out depends on your own natural hair hue, your color history, and how your hair reacts to the process—not to mention how pictures can betray reality.

For any service your colorist recommends, ask about the cost of that service, the cost and frequency of any touch-ups required to maintain the color, and your aftercare regimen. Definitely let your colorist know how much aftercare you're willing to commit to before he or she does anything. You also have to be honest about your hair color history, because that has a direct impact on the finish of your new color. Whether you're a virgin head of hair, you've dabbled with at-home hair color, or you've been through more than your fair share of colorists in

Top Trick

If you swim in salt or chlorinated water with color-treated hair, your color will fade much more quickly. But there's an easy-to-do top trick to prevent this: The hair shaft can absorb only so much water, so thoroughly rinse your hair in the shower before diving in. Your hair will have absorbed all the water it can before salt or chlorine can cause color-fading damage. Do that and there's nothing to worry about.

the past, come clean, because knowing your color history increases your stylist's chances of success tenfold. Even if you had a few highlights a year ago and they've since faded away and been replaced with a new allover single-process color, your colorist needs to know about the highlights so he or she can more accurately predict how the new color will react to any previous processes.

With all these elements to talk about, a color consultation can last a bit longer than a cut consultation—up to about ten minutes is normal. But the same basic ideas apply: You should be exchanging thoughts, color suggestions, and history with your colorist, and he or she should also display an awareness of any potential problems as well as talk about your aftercare process. Make sure you feel calm, comfortable, and confident, like you're with a great professional colorist who, for the length of your stay, is dedicated to you and your needs.

If he or she hasn't already asked, let your

colorist know whether you are looking for a temporary or permanent change, allover color, or a few highlights; whether you want an elegant, refined change, or a bold, dramatic statement. Once your color history, your commitment to color, and what sort of color service you want have been established, talk with your colorist about the shades and tones that will work best for you, your hair, and your level of commitment. Once you're confident and happy with the exchange of ideas and have mutually agreed upon a direction, you're ready to take the plunge.

Color is a key component of a successful hairstyle, and if you're having your color done at a salon, finding a great colorist is the key to successful color. But how do you know when you've got a great colorist? First and foremost, the new color, and your colorist, should make you look and feel fantastic. Also pay attention to how long your color holds up after your appointment. With reasonable aftercare, good

single-process color retains its luster for a minimum of four weeks, and, if the hair is healthy, six weeks and more. Highlights should define your look for a minimum of two months before needing a redo.

Besides how your color looks and lasts, there are a couple of telltale signs that will help you separate the brilliant colorists from the okay colorists. All good colorists should write down your formula for future reference. Make sure yours does this, so that at your next appointment, when you talk about how the color worked for you or how you may like to refine it, the colorist can look at the formula and modify it according to your wishes.

Also, when you get a touch-up on the regrowth of a single-process hair color, unskilled professionals can leave an unsightly band of color. This happens when they don't color all the way to the color line in the hair, leaving you with an ugly band of mismatched color. Watch for this; if it's prominent, speak to your colorist about it first. If he or she can't fix the problem, go to someone who can.

Client Color Q & A

Although I am professionally trained in cutting and coloring, cutting hair is my specialty. In the salon, I leave all hair coloring to my world-class team of colorists, while I concentrate on cutting those luscious locks! In this chapter I've drawn on their experience and expertise because they are the ones coloring clients every day. One guy who helped me a huge amount was James Edick. James has been working with me since I first opened up my own salon and he colors the hair of all my clients while also traveling with me to hair shows and seminars around the world. When we sat down to talk, some key client questions kept coming up. Here are the questions and what James had to say about them.

What effect does well water have on my hair?

This is a common question. Since well water is better to drink, some clients believe it's also better for their hair. Unfortunately, if you have hair color, that's not the case. If you regularly wash your hair in well water, the extra minerals can cause color to fade. It can change the hair texture a bit, too, making it drier and more brittle or softer and flatter, depending on what minerals are in the water. Don't worry too much about salons having well water. If they do, they know about it and account for it in the color process. If you have well water at home and are concerned that showering in it is going to weaken your hair color, you can buy a showerhead filter that takes out the minerals. These cost between $50 and $100.

I have highlights, and I when I comb my hair I can see uneven stripes at the roots and on my scalp. Why is that?

These often look like tiger stripes of uneven color; technically they're known as bleed marks.

There are a few ways this can happen: The color may not have been mixed correctly, the highlights may have been applied too close to the scalp, the foils or packets may not have

The red isn't visible (unless you want it to be), but it stops the hair from turning green; if your colorist fails to add in the red, then going green is a possibility. Finally, if you've been swimming without a cap, salt or chlorine can also turn colored hair green, especially if you're colored blond or bleach blond. If this happens to you, getting a new salon color is a surefire route to success, but deep, clarifying shampoos, available from salons, beauty supply houses, and drug-stores, also help. Better yet, most salons offer clarifying treatments, which are more effective (but also more expensive) than the at-home clarifying shampoos.

> f you really want your eyebrows colored—if your hair is light blond and your brows are very dark brown, for example—go to an aesthetician.

been applied properly, or, if you wash your hair in well water, the minerals may have caused uneven fading. The best way to fix this is to go back to the salon and ask your colorist to weave in some subtle lowlights. This blends out any mismatched highlighting.

Why does my hair color turn green, and what can I do about it?

The most common reason for hair color turning green is that the water you shampoo and rinse with contains copper. You'll know because any metal surfaces in your bath, shower, or sink will also turn green if the water has copper in it. It is also possible that your colorist used the wrong formula when taking your hair from light to dark. Going light to dark involves using ash tones, which can turn green in time. To prevent this, a good colorist uses tints of red to balance it out.

Should I color my eyebrows?

We advise our clients not to do this. For a start, the eyebrows grow quickly and you'll soon be seeing your natural color growing in anyway. Also, there are active chemicals in hair color. They are dangerous to the eyes, and the eyebrows are just too close for comfort. It's far better to wear eye shadow, which is safer and can be changed according to your mood and inclination. If you really want your eyebrows colored—if your hair is light blond and your brows are very dark brown, for example—go to an aesthetician. Aestheticians are licensed in this field and the chemicals they use are less harmful. Ask your stylist to recommend a good one, or look up the best spas in your area on www.citysearch.com.

How many colors could/should I have in my highlights?

It is a good idea to go for multiple-color level highlighting, commonly referred to as multidimensional highlights. These tend to look more natural, and as the hair and the highlights grow out, they continue to look soft and wholesome. Single-color highlights can look a bit harsh as they grow out. Going for three different color levels is a good bet. You could have one highlight that is one level lighter than your natural color, then another two or three levels lighter, and another three or four levels lighter. Otherwise, go for one level of lowlighting and two levels of highlights. That looks great, too, with lots of added depth and dimension.

What should I expect when going from a light to dark hair color?

Often when a client has colored her hair lighter and she later wants to go back to her natural, darker, hair color, she finds that the new dark color is too strong and a bit of a shock. This happens because clients generally look only at the ends of their hair, and they forget how dark their natural hair color was. Take baby steps and go halfway toward your natural color. This won't be such a big shock and then, if you want to, you can go back to the salon a few weeks down the line and complete the job. This is better for your hair. Going from light to a bit darker and

then a bit darker again is a much simpler process than going from light to dark and then back to light again, which is a lot of work and places unnecessary stress on the hair.

Building a Color Relationship

Because of the potential hazards, and because of the intricate, artistic nature of hair color, where mistakes can ruin the integrity of the hair and an off tone can damage personal style, once clients finds a colorist they like and who knows their color history and formula, they tend to stick by that colorist for many years. It's well-known in the industry that clients show more loyalty to their colorist than to their haircutter (although some stylists work in both fields, and the cutter and colorist are sometimes the same person). For these reasons, it's critical to build a great relationship with your colorist.

Find a person who's talented, whom you can communicate with, and who does the right things for *you*—encourages you to color within your natural parameters; explains what will and won't work for you, your hair, and your skin tone; discusses with you your color history and commitment to aftercare; and gives you lustrous, contemporary color that lasts.

If your colorist does these things, even if the first time your color isn't your perfect dream, then it's still worth investing the time to build a relationship. It can take a few tries to get color exactly right, and over time you and your colorist can refine your formula into that perfect hair color for you.

Aftercare

Now that you've got great hair color, your priority is the right aftercare regimen to maintain that bright new hue. You need to nurture your hair after a color process because coloring can leave the scalp irritated and the hair swollen with the cuticle layers left open (when we apply color, the chemical process opens up the cuticle), which results in moisture loss and, of course, fading.

The first step is to wait at least twenty-four hours after your color treatment before you shampoo and condition your hair. Just after your color has been applied is the most vulnerable period for hair color. If you shampoo and condition too soon, before the hair cuticle has had time to close, locking in the color molecule, then fading can be a problem.

Next, you should switch to protective color-safe shampoos and conditioners. These products have tiny tints of color in them, which help to retain vivid and long-lasting blushes of color in your hair. In today's marketplace, no matter what color palette you go for, there are products tailored exactly to you. For blondes and bleach blondes, blond color-savers reduce the brassy yellowing effect common when blondes start to fade, reviving dull and lackluster hair. Specialist color-saver shampoos and conditioners are also available for all shades of red, black, and brown hair, and using these products regularly encourages lasting, natural-looking color. You can shampoo and condition at the same intervals as you would normally, although again I suggest conditioning more than you shampoo because the added moisture in the conditioners is a big aid against the drying effects of hair color. Another good idea—and practically essential if you've gone bleach blond—is a once-weekly deep-conditioning treatment. There are loads of these types of products in salons and in your local beauty supply store. Normally they're designed to be left on the hair for twenty or thirty minutes and provide a feast of moisture for undernourished and overprocessed hair.

Environmental elements can also induce fading, so if you're basking in the sun a lot, those heat rays will definitely start to pull out the color pigment. Of course the foolproof method to counter this is to wear a hat or scarf. If that's not an option for you—at least not every day—styling products that contain UV protection block the sun's damaging effect on your hair, just as sunscreen prevents damage to your skin. These products are also readily available in your local salon or beauty supply store.

The heat of blow-dryers and hot irons is another concern for color-treated hair. As you know, adding color tends to dry out your hair, and these hot tools can dry it out even more. The combined effect can cause brittle and porous hair where the color badly fades. So go easy on heat tools, try not to use them every day, condition often (almost every day if you can), and apply thermal protectors before you start styling.

At-Home Hair Color

The fundamental difference between doing it yourself or at the salon is that a salon colorist is a professional, someone you can trust to impartially assess what's right for you. With at-home color, you put your trust in a box. The box doesn't know your normal hair color or what processes it's been through over time. There's no way of knowing how the box of color will react with your hair until you've tried it. You are taking a risk by putting your hair in your own hands. If you don't like the cost of salon hair color, color from a box is an option, but keep in mind that if you don't like the results, it's even harder for you to correct the color.

If you do try at-home color, remember that color doesn't shift color, so if you don't like the results, going immediately to the salon for color correction isn't your best option. You are much better off waiting a few weeks for the color to fade. Be sure to let any professional colorist know about all at-home color processes you have undertaken in the past.

My advice: If you want a great color but don't want to part with the cash, then go to a top-end salon and ask to be a model as part of their training program. Most high-quality salons have great education programs and the apprentices are normally young, very talented and creative people who are eager to impress by giving you great service. The consultation and service will take longer than normal because it is a training exercise. Expect a senior staff member to regularly check your colorist's work. Overall, it's a great option—the chance to get professional color for not much money, normally no more than $30.

For those of you who do want to dabble in at-home color, no problem. My mom still does it to this day, and I experimented with it as a teenager. I've learned a lot since then, so let's look at some ways you can increase your chances of success.

Pick the right process. The same manufacturers that make salon colors also make the at-home color boxes, so the quality of the color is not a major issue (it's the fact that you have an experienced color professional taking care of you in the salon that is the major difference) and there are semi-, demi-, and permanent colors available. This isn't always labeled on the box, though, so here's the secret: Semipermanent comes ready to go in a tube while demi- and permanent color need to be mixed by you. You already know that semi is less damaging than permanent; also, if you don't get the mixing process right, this is another way your at-home color can go wrong. For those two reasons, if you're worried about potential damage, err on the side of caution and go for a semipermanent at-home color. If you choose a demi- or a permanent self-mixed color, always follow the instructions to the letter.

Pick the right color. My advice: Consider your natural color level and go for a color that is a shade or two lighter rather than a shade or two darker. Staying close to your base color is a huge advantage for at-home color. In addition, if things go wrong, it's much easier for a professional colorist to color your hair back to dark than to color it back to light. Home highlighting systems are too tricky and risky to be performed at home. It's far better to go for an all-over color that is close to your natural shade.

Application tips. For the application, all you can do is follow the guidelines on the box. It would certainly help to have a friend with you to make sure you have distributed the color thoroughly and evenly. Even better, she could apply the color for you.

Touch-ups. If you find an at-home color you like and want to continue your at-home hair color journey, I advise sticking with that same color. As I've already mentioned, finding a perfect color is a tough challenge, so once you do it's a good idea to maintain it. When you start to feel that your hair color is looking dull, without the shimmer and shine you're used to, simply buy the same box of color from the same manufacturer to reinvigorate your look.

My Key Color Thoughts

- Keep it simple. The more complex, the more things can go wrong. And repairing bad color is one of the toughest challenges for even the world's great colorists. Go gently, and think about how far you can go without risking the integrity of your hair.

- On the color-levels chart, always stay within three to four levels of your natural color.

- A subtle combination of highlights in two or three compatible colors creates incredible dimension, a beautiful effect, and a detailed look of quality, all without the commitment of a full single process.

- Embrace color—it's an awesome way to enhance your look and define your personality.

- Get a color that complements your natural features and shines through long into the night.

- If you've got long hair and you love it long, great—you don't need a big change in your cut to change your look. Color it and you get that revitalizing sense of renewal without losing the length.

- How color reacts on your hair also depends on what work has previously taken place. Virgin heads—heads with no previous hair color—always turn out the best. If this is you, you have a great opportunity, but start slowly and see how it goes.

- If you're growing out color, put a demi- or semipermanent color into your roots to mask the unsightly regrowth. This keeps you looking great, and it soon fades or washes away, allowing you to go back to your natural color without any problems.

- After four to six weeks, single-process color begins to fade. If you want to keep the same dynamic hue, it's time for a redo to keep your color looking gorgeous.

- Color is expensive, and that's why you should recognize exactly what you need and get that done—nothing more. If you have longer hair and you've recently had highlights, you can just do a half head of highlights. That glosses over the top half of your hair and gives you enough shine, color, and gloss to still get compliments on your color.

- If your hair is light and you want to go lighter, I recommend golden tones, because gold gives you more light reflection and, consequently, more shimmer and shine.

- As we age, our skin color becomes paler. You need to think about this with regard to hair color. As your skin tone lightens, so should your hair color. If you keep your color the same as you age, it will eventually make you look pale. Lighten the color to soften your features.

- Always follow a color treatment with aftercare. Color-safe shampoos and conditioners are a must, and if you're in the sun a lot, so are hats, scarves, and UV-formulated styling aids.

- Don't follow celebrities too closely for their hair color. You can use them for inspiration and ideas, but remember they have top stylists with them all day every day. Sure, they can go from black to blond in an instant, and so could you if you had a team of stylists working on your hair every single day. But since you don't, get hair color that works for you.

Summing It All Up

In "Great Hair Color," I've shown you how hair color can change, revitalize, and individualize your identity.

You can make hair color succeed for you by using the level system. This is your guide to how much lighter and how much darker you can take your hair color and still stay within the natural parameters of natural-looking, healthy hair. The level system also shows you what you need to do if you want to break these natural parameters for a more radical color change. If you're a rare natural redhead, you know you need to speak to your colorist to determine the right hair color for you.

Whatever color you choose, you can pick warm or cool tones according to your personal preferences. This may change with trends, too, and you should watch for changes of direction in color trends through magazines, TV, and film. Even better, ask your colorist what are the most up-to-date styles and you're sure to stay current. As a rule of thumb, go lighter in summer and darker in winter, but don't follow color trends religiously, especially if the hot colors of the season just don't feel right for you. Use hair color to enhance *your* look. Make it a style-defining part of *your* lifestyle and personality first; follow fashion second. Keep in mind the full range of hair color options as well: Semi-permanent, demipermanent, permanent, and the bleach and tone all have different features and benefits, as do the different salon service options: highlights, lowlights, slicing, and single-process hair color. Pick the right match for your level of commitment to color.

Remember the importance of a great color consultation and work to build and keep a long-term relationship with your colorist. Color is a tricky process and if you work together, the formula can be refined over time to find the perfect color for you. If you color your hair, be sure to use the right aftercare regimen to retain the luster in your hue—color-safe shampoos and conditioners are a must.

If you're into at-home hair color, always play it safe by going a shade or two lighter than your natural level. And when you find an at-home color you love, stick with it!

Embrace great hair color because it lifts your look, and your spirit.

7. Problem Hair and Maintenance

've come across all types of problem hair over the years. From wild, flyaway hair, to thick, unmanageable locks, to out-of-control curls—you name it, I've seen it. I've also seen clients with all types of troublesome hair making some of the most adventurous requests of their hairdressers, requests that would definitely make you laugh—or cry.

I'll never forget the woman with thinning hair—50 percent of it was already all gone—who wanted a long, flowing, and shapely Farrah Fawcett style. What could I say? "Sorry, love, but you're never going to look like a Charlie's Angel," was my opening gambit!

When I first moved to New York, the "Rachel" (Jennifer Aniston's haircut from the early days of *Friends*) was oh-so-hot-to-trot. But it wasn't right for everybody, especially the woman with superthick, supertight spiral-shaped curls who politely asked me to make her look "just like Jennifer." "Absolutely, love. Now where did I put that nuclear-strength straightening iron?"

This isn't the right way to start every consultation, but sometimes a gag, or a loose, casual, and jokey tone helps break the ice with a nervous or unsure client. I use what I need to, even the cheeky side of my personality, to help me and the client get where we need to,

especially when the client has real problem hair and is having trouble facing reality.

The reality is this: If you have extreme natural frizz, supertight curly hair, sun-damaged or overprocessed hair, thinning hair, or extrathick wirelike hair, then styling your hair can be a real battle. I say "can," because it doesn't have to be that way. You know by now that my philosophy is to choose styles, techniques, and products that are going to work for your hair type, because this makes it much easier to achieve quick and easy success from day to day. If you have problem hair, you need to be even more committed to following these guidelines. Your options are more limited, because, as your hair is so extreme, the more you try to take it away from its natural state, the more unmanageable it becomes. That's why I had to start those two lovely ladies off with a joke. I had to get them back to reality because they were asking for styles that were so far removed from what they could easily achieve that their hair would have

turned into a real nightmare. Maybe if I had summoned all my experience and skill, I could have got somewhere near the styles they wanted, but they would have looked totally unnatural, and day-to-day styling would have certainly driven them to drink.

If you have problem hair, there's little point in cursing your rotten luck. Your hair is what it is and it's part of who you are. Besides, remember what I said in the beginning: Even the most crazy, wild, out-of-control hair can look gorgeous if you start with the right cut and then use the right products and techniques to retain the integrity of your hair. Be realistic about what your hair can achieve and accept that there are certain maintenance routines that you need to adopt, and I promise you healthy, sexy, minimal-fuss hair that is sure to make you one hot mama.

Now let's talk about how to maintain and style all kinds of so-called problem hair. I'll recommend some haircuts from my style guide that will be the best fit for you.

Extremely Frizzy Hair

Extreme natural frizz normally occurs in hair that has a tough, coarse texture. The hair is usually very dry and very curly (although, rarely, extreme natural frizzy hair can be seen in straighter hair types). It's also common in gray hair, because as hair ages and becomes increasingly gray, the texture grows increasingly coarse and frizzy. Your primary difficulty is managing your hair from day to day because even moisture-based leave-in conditioners or curl and styling crèmes are likely to leave your hair dry, frizzy, and separated with no true sense of style.

Your number one priority is to get the right haircut. A strong (rather than a soft) shape is much easier to maintain on a daily basis. The round two and a half inches (page 64) or any cut that is short to midlength with a good solid shape perfectly suits extremely frizzy (either curly, straight, or gray) hair. These cuts don't alter your hair texture, but the strong shapes get you looking polished and pulled together, and controlling frizz is much more manageable, making your styling quick and simple.

When it comes to styling, a silicone-based defrizz serum should become your best friend. If you're curly and frizzy, use the smoothing properties of silicone defrizz along with a moisture-based grooming or curl crème to lock in curls without the dryness and without the frizz. You should definitely try my controlled curls styling technique on page 113. Master this technique on a strong-shaped haircut and you'll have an easy frizz-free look you'll love. If you're one of the rare straight-hair frizzies or have gray hair with extreme frizz, I recommend using a defrizz serum with a styling crème or smoothing lotion to slick the hair down. Try the smooth blow-out styling technique highlighted on page 109. Curly, straight, or gray superfrizzy types can also all try the wraparound technique illustrated on page 102—all hair is smoother when you use this brilliant and easy technique.

My top-tip method for adding moisture to dry, frizzy hair is a bit of an old salon secret that has unfortunately been nearly forgotten over the years. I've yet to see any newfangled trick or product work as brilliantly as this very effective technique: Once a week, pack a hairnet with a light leave-in conditioner. Use three to four times more product than normal and put the hairnet over your wet to damp hair for ten minutes. This is a great way to lock the moisture-giving benefits of the product in to the hair shaft for added support. After ten minutes, take off the hairnet but avoid the temptation to rinse out the product—leave it in. Your hair will be richly moisturized, soft, smooth, shiny, and have more malleability, making it much easier for you to style. You can even add a little styling crème into the hairnet mix to give your hair added textural support for styling.

Finally, when you're not packing your hair with leave-in conditioner, you should regularly use a moisturizing shampoo and moisturizing conditioner that penetrate into the hair shaft. This gives your hair essential day-to-day moisture support.

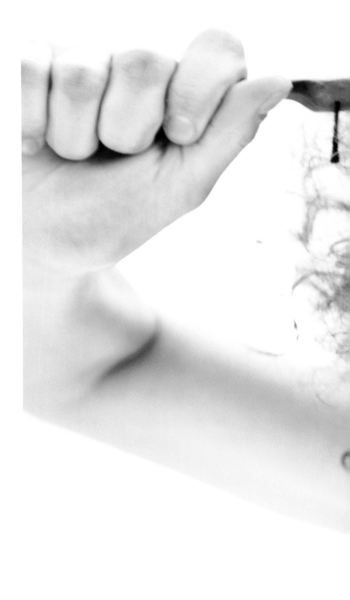

Extreme and Unmanageable Supercurly Hair

Supercurly hair shrinks up into tight ringlet-style spirals. It looks dense and it's difficult to see the definition of your curls because they're packed

so tightly together. The hair texture can be either very fine or very thick, but the density is generally very heavy. The combination of a very rounded curly hair shape and a dense head of hair makes most people with this hair type feel like there's nothing they can do.

Get the right haircut and there's *a lot* you can do. You need a cut that celebrates the curl. A shorter cut (especially if your hair likes to puff up and out, which is likely if the texture is thick) that creates pieciness and separation in the length is your ideal. One of my favorites is the rounded graduation (page 67), and you can also try the round one inch (page 65) and the round two and a half inches (page 64). These cuts give you greater dimension, your look will be strong, and it will be easier for you to control your hair.

A great, easy styling idea is to blow-dry the front straight. Just apply a defrizz serum to

blend of the straighter shape at the front and the more curly sections at the back, and you're golden. And because you're styling only your bangs, this technique is quick and simple. The rest can dry naturally—although I advise scrunching in some leave-in conditioner to the tips, just to soften them up.

To get shapely curls all over, you can use my controlled curls styling technique (page 113). If you prefer to go straighter and smoother, use a defrizz serum, the high heat of a blow-dryer, and a boar-bristle brush (the most effective smoothing brush) with my smooth blow-out technique (page 109) to flatten out and soften up your hair as much as possible.

Whether your supercurly hair texture is fine or thick, you don't need to shampoo your hair nearly as much as you need to condition. Your hair is much better off if you get into the rinse-and-condition habit, rather than the shampoo-and-condition habit. Don't worry about dirt; the oils from your scalp don't run through this hair type so much because it's so dense, and whatever natural oils do come through actually aid your natural texture and make your hair more manageable. Using a moisture-rich conditioner is,

> Whether your supercurly hair texture is fine or thick, you don't need to shampoo your hair nearly as much as you need to condition.

damp bangs and blow-dry with a round brush on mid-to-high heat. In about two minutes your hair will be smoother and more polished in the front, while the rest of your hair remains naturally curly. Just make sure you create a nice even

on the other hand, essential. Extremely curly hair is almost always dry, and you need that added moisture to fight the frizz. As a general rule, shampoo once a week, condition each and every day.

Sun-Damaged Hair

The heat of the sun's rays has the power to cause damage. It can cause tangles, make split ends more noticeable, and cause color to fade. Ultimately, you'll be able to feel how dehydrated, damaged, and brittle your hair has become.

Of course, my best advice is to prevent your hair from becoming sun damaged in the first place. Whenever you're in the sun, you should protect your hair the same way as you protect your skin. Nowadays, you can find shampoos, conditioners, and styling products with UV protection in your local hair salon or beauty supply store, and you should use one or more of these products for any extended periods of time in the sun.

Even better, wear a hat or scarf. These can look supercool, and covering up is the best sun-protection method there is. Also, remember that if you're vacationing, you can wear your hair more casual than usual. There's no need to blow it out so often, thus subjecting it to heat stress as well as sun stress. Pull it back into a low pony and you're good to go. The added glow the sun gives your skin means you don't have to rely so much on your hair to add that final polish to your look, not to mention the fact that your vacation should be about being laid back and having a good time, not about hair styling.

If you're on vacation, there's a good chance you'll be near the sea, and the salt water it's filled with, so let's talk about that, too: Salt water does put some interesting and pretty-looking textures into your hair, but it's also extremely drying and likely to cause damage, especially when combined with the sun's heat rays. If you're heading into the ocean, remember these two words: moisturizing conditioner. Normally you rinse out moisturizing conditioner, but on this occasion, leaving a moisture-based conditioner in your hair before bathing in salt water—or, indeed, chlorine-filled water—gives you an essential moisture-filled barrier of protection.

If your hair has already been shattered by the sun, a deep-conditioning, keratin-based treatment can help (see "Overprocessed Hair" on the following page for more details on this). But if the ends are truly split, get a cut. It's the only way to get back your hair's health and luster.

Humidity Hair

In England, humidity hair is not really much of a problem, and I heard very little about it until I made my move to the States, where the hot, sticky summer climate definitely does cause real problems, especially for curly hair. That's chiefly because curly hair is the driest hair type, and dry hair is attracted to the added moisture in the air. This can cause unwanted and unruly fullness and frizz for anyone whose hair is on the dry side (which can include straighter hair types as well). The problem is that when your dry hair attracts the extra moisture in the air, it begins to swell. If you don't do anything to protect yourself, the humidity makes your hair expand, expand, and expand until any styling you've done goes by the wayside and is replaced by uncontrollable volume, or curl, or frizz, or, in some cases, all three.

If heat-humidity is causing problems for you, here are some steps you can take to minimize its effect on your hairstyle:

First of all, throughout the hot summer months, switch to a rich moisturizing, hydrating, or clarifying conditioner. The added moisture these types of conditioners put into your hair helps keep the added moisture in the air from seeping into the hair shaft. How? Simply put, if your hair has enough moisture in it to begin with, it will not swell up looking for the additional moisture in the atmosphere.

If your hair is straight to moderately wavy, it's also essential to use a high-quality defrizz serum that fights the frizz throughout the day.

Remember, with defrizz serum, you focus the application from the midlengths to the ends, and you also need to blow-dry on a high heat to get the maximum benefits from the product. Curly hair types should focus on the controlled curls styling technique on page 113. This gives you beautifully defined curls that stand a great chance of holding up to the humidity. And for both curly and straighter hair types that suffer in the humidity, it's essential to put a moisturizing styling product in your purse and carry it with you all day. You can use a leave-in conditioner, a moisture-based hair crème, or a hair refresher when you feel your hair starting to puff up and out. Just apply a small pea-sized amount of the product to the hair to add moisture. This freshens up your hair and provides a layer of protection to fight the humidity.

Also, it's vital on days like these that you don't fight your hair too much. If your hair is straight, wear it straight rather than trying to make it wavy or curly; if your hair is wavy, wear it wavy rather than trying to make it straight or curly; and if your hair is curly, wear it curly rather than trying to make it straight. I say this because humidity tends to return your hair to its natural state, so trying to fight it by styling against your natural shape and texture only makes it much, much worse. Keeping it natural gives you the best chance to maintain a humidity-free look.

Finally, I will talk about ionic technology later in this chapter, which is something you should definitely investigate for yourself. Ionic styling tools stand up better to humidity than their traditional counterparts.

Overprocessed Hair

Overprocessed hair has been put under heavy stress. Signs of overprocessing include hair that is falling out at a rapid rate, dry, brittle hair, and split ends. These problems stem from too much chemical color work, too much permanent waving, and/or too much straightening or curling with a hot iron.

Hair like this needs lots more care and lots more moisture to get it back into tip-top shape. Use a rich moisturizing shampoo and conditioner to pack in the moisture and take extra

> For both curly and straighter hair types that suffer in the humidity, it's essential to put a moisturizing styling product in your purse and carry it with you all day.

time to condition your ends thoroughly. Use moisture-based styling products like crèmes and lotions as well and be extra careful with your hair every day. Stay away from extensive

blow-drying and heat tools whenever possible because they add more stress.

I also recommend a once-weekly keratin-based treatment. (I recommended this as a method of prevention, too, especially if your hair isn't overprocessed yet, but you like to go to town with your heat tools.) Keratin is a strong, tough protein, and it's a major component of your hair shaft. So when the keratin dies away, as it does especially quickly in overprocessed hair, your hair becomes increasingly dry and brittle. Adding layers of keratin builds protein-filled molecules in your hair shaft. It won't make your hair feel soft and silky, but it will strengthen it, and that reduces breakage. If you feel your hair could do with this type of strengthening, ask your salon stylist to recommend the right keratin-based products for you.

Another problem with overprocessed hair is that it's difficult to color successfully because

your hair becomes like a fragile fabric and the color molecules just don't lock properly into the hair shaft. The chances of a successful color service decrease tenfold on overprocessed hair. If you're in this overprocessed scenario but feel in desperate need of a new style-defining hue, the best thing to do is get a trim before you get the color. Damage in overprocessed hair always begins at the tips of the shaft because that's the oldest part of your hair. In fact, hair never gets damaged in the middle or at the roots before it gets damaged at the ends. Cutting off most of the damage (rarely does the damage spread far up the hair shaft) allows your bright new color to take full effect.

Finally, I recommend that anyone with overprocessed hair get a cut or trim, even if you're not thinking of a color service. This is the best way to get back the vital healthy-looking luster that makes any shape or style look so much better.

Thinning Hair

Thinning hair is a problem for many women. The thought of major hair loss is, understandably, a subject of much worry and angst, but before you panic, remember these few simple things:

Hair loss can be sporadic, and there are times when we all go through more shedding than usual. Typically, new hair follicles grow in every seven years, replacing the older ones. Anytime you start to shed more hair than normal, it may well be a part of your natural cycle.

Postpregnancy, a lot of women encounter hair loss. The most common period of hair loss occurs around three months after delivery. The rise in hormones during pregnancy keeps you from losing your hair. After delivery, the hormones return to normal levels, which allows the hair to fall out and return to the normal cycle. The normal hair loss that was delayed during pregnancy may fall out all at once, causing worry about long-term thinning of the hair. However, between six and twelve months after giving birth, hair growth returns to normal.

With longer hair and curly hair, the typical hundred hairs a day that fall out of everybody's hair often get trapped in the scalp and come out only when you wash or brush your hair. So if you see lots of hair on your brush or in your shower, it may well be residual fallen-out hair.

Stress, health, and diet all play a part in thinning-out hair. So eat healthy and be well for thick luscious locks!

Medical hair-growth treatments can and do work for some, but to keep up the hair growth you have to keep up the treatments for life. So before you start down this road, be sure that you are prepared for the lifelong commitment.

It's very, very rare for a woman to look truly balding without having alopecia. Alopecia is a medical condition that requires treatment by a physician. Otherwise, baldness is something for men to worry about, not you.

Nobody's hair is as thick as it was in her youth. As we age, we get wrinkles and our skin loses its elasticity. *And* as we age, our hair begins to thin out, too.

Having said all that, if your hair is anywhere between superfine and floppy to noticeably translucent, your focus should be on getting a shorter, more textured hairstyle. This is, without a doubt, essential for thinner hair types. If your hair is thin in density, fine, and light, a short haircut allows the hairs to sit on top of one another and gives you that vital illusion of thickness (as opposed to a long hairstyle, which hangs straight down and consequently appears even finer and thinner). You'll lose that feeling of thin hair, and you'll be more comfortable with your locks. Layering your short hair adds to the illusion of thickness. Try the light face-frame cut

(page 40), the bob cut (page 36), or the shag cut (page 37)—all are short enough to allow your hairs to sit happily on top of one another. Go for bangs, too. This allows you to style your hair forward instead of brushing it back. Bringing your hair forward is another excellent way to give the illusion of thickness; brush or slick it back and thinness becomes much more visible.

To cleanse and condition really fine hair, use the lightest daily shampoo and the lightest daily conditioner you can find. Thicker moisturizing products weigh your hair down into a flat and floppy look. There are now shampoos and conditioners on the market labeled "volumizing," "thickening," or something similar. The intention is to puff out the hair molecule for fullness. Results vary from person to person, but they are worth a try. If this new technology works for you, great, but whatever shampoo and conditioner you use, you need only a bit. That's especially true with conditioner, because too much makes your fine, fragile hair too soft and unable to maintain any style-defining structure. And remember to rinse out cleansing and conditioning products extra well. Any residue on such fine hair weighs it down even more.

For styling, volumizing foam is your number one go-to product. This helps you to build density, texture, and dimension. But remember, finer, thinner hair doesn't need too much product; again, it weighs it down. Apply a small amount at the roots and blow-dry using the volumizing technique (page 107); this is a great way to add more thickness, structure, and volume to any hairstyle.

People with thinner hair types also need to be careful with hair color, especially if your hair is so thin that it is translucent through to the scalp. Why? Because your scalp has a light hue, and a dark hair color provides a contrast that showcases the prominence of your scalp. On the other hand, a lighter hair color helps to disguise any see-through areas.

Extrathick, Coarse, and Wirelike Tough-to-Manage Hair

People with extrathick wirelike hair have up to three hairs in each hair follicle and are also likely to have a lower hairline—one that encroaches on your forehead and sits low down on the nape of your neck. It's infuriatingly tough to manage hair like this because it's so dense, thick, and coarse that it's difficult to get a brush or product to go through the hair.

Once again, the cut you get is all-important. Go for a style two inches or shorter in length with lots of texture, and it's much easier to control your hair. Or choose a shoulder-length or longer style and let the added weight help pull your hair straight down, also making it easier to manage. Additionally, with a longer style, you can pull your hair back into a ponytail, which, of course, is something anybody can do. For a shorter cut, try the cropped razor cut (page 51) or the graduated razor cut (page 46). Or, to go longer, the two long layered cuts (pages 56 and 58) make your day-to-day styling that much easier.

You need the right products, too. Oil-based, moisture-rich styling crèmes and lotions make managing your hair easier. To smooth it out, blow-dry using a defrizz serum with a flat paddle brush. Or substitute a straightening iron for the flat paddle brush for maximum smoothness and softness. (Remember the one bonus of thick coarse hair: It's so strong and so tough that it can take lots of heat tools without becoming damaged.) Read over my instructions for the smooth blow out (page 109) and flat iron forward (page 111). With either technique, the heat helps to press your hair flat, leaving it straight and smooth, which is exactly what you want to achieve with such thick and puffy hair texture.

This is another hair type that you should refrain from shampooing too much. Even shampooing once every two or three weeks is enough because the natural oils from your scalp don't run through your hair (because it's so thick and dense) and make it dirty as they do in other hair types. Besides, very clean, coarse hair puffs up and out more, the opposite of what you want. Focus on conditioning instead. Use a deep or moisturizing conditioner thoroughly and often to condition the midsection through to the ends of your hair. Extracoarse hair is typically very dry, so adding moisture instantly makes it easier to shape and define your style because your hair is that much more malleable.

Rarely, when the hair texture is unbelievably thick and dense, no amount of moisture-based conditioners, defrizz serums, or heat tools can make the out-of-control, unmanageable thickness go away. I sympathize—this can cause a lot of heartache. The best thing you can do is invest in thermal reconditioning. This is normally how ethnic hair types "relax" their own unique and challenging hair, but it also smoothes out extrathick Caucasian and Latina hair. It costs a lot—between $500 and $1,000 per treatment—and you need to keep it up (twice a year, in most cases), but it leaves your hair permanently flat, smooth, and straight (only your new growth hair continues to grow back in a thick, unmanageable way). Never do this on fine or overprocessed hair—it'll just break off. I absolutely insist that you go to a true expert with extensive experience in the field, because even on strong, thick, and coarse hair, if it's done incorrectly your hair will break off. No cheap tricksters or charlatans, please! (To find out more about thermal reconditioning, go to page 207.)

All Other Problems

If you're free of all the specific problems outlined in this chapter, and yet you still feel like you're fighting your hair, then you should take a fresh look at yourself. Go to your hairdresser and ask what's the best look you can achieve with the minimal maintenance and styling effort. You may also want to consider making an additional investment by going to see a highly skilled and experienced professional. The art director, education director, or salon owner of a locally or world-renowned salon may cost that much more, but if you go only once, it may be worth it. Ask the professional for his or her expert advice and then get a great cut that you love and can maintain and style easily. After the first great cut, you know what works for you and are in a better position to ask another, less expensive stylist to repeat, or come close to repeating, the same style.

With the help of this book, I hope I've shattered the bad-hair day myth. Still, we all have days when bits of hair tend to defy our every styling attempt. On days like these, use accessories such as pony bands, bobby pins, clips, and grips to keep hair in good working order. I love these devices; they're incredibly feminine and can accessorize any look perfectly, while also helping to tame any problem areas. (If you need more help on how to use these accessories best, then have a fresh look at "Pin Basics" and "Pin Perfect" on pages 123 and 230.)

Maintaining Gorgeous Hair for All Hair Types

Aside from the specific cuts and techniques I've outlined for successful style in all types of problem hair, I want to give you general guidelines for gorgeous, healthy hair no matter what your hair type. And I also want to talk about certain products and tools that have huge benefits for day-to-day styling.

Great Hair comes from working with the natural texture of your hair, getting a great cut

> Stay away from blow-drying on high heat unless that's absolutely necessary for you, and buy heat tools with a temperature gauge.

that's a match for you *and* your hair texture and shape, the right shampoo and conditioner regimen, and easy, effective styling using the proper products and tools. I love working with hair, and I hope, with the help of this book, you will, too. Have a blast finding out how different styling techniques and different products work for you, but keep your hair free from abuse. Go easy on the heat tools, and when you do use them, take precautions (see "Thermal Protectors," below). Stay away from blow-drying on high heat unless that's absolutely necessary for you, and buy heat tools with a temperature gauge and use it to keep the temperature as low as possible.

THERMAL PROTECTORS

A thermal protector spray, lotion, or crème is essential for anyone who regularly uses heat tools. It massively reduces the damage to your hair by forming a protective barrier against the heat. You still need your existing styling product wonderfully effective. The price you pay, however, is heat-induced damage to your hair. Sure, you look great today and tomorrow, but constant use can and does cause real damage to the hair shaft. When that happens, it's really tough to get your hair looking good, no matter what cut you have, or what product or tool you are using. I've already talked about how thermal protectors are essential if you want to use heat tools regularly, but I want to give you some additional

Keep your heat tools moving as much as possible, no more than fifteen or twenty seconds before moving on to the next section.

(volumizing foam, styling crème, defrizz serum, and so on), and the best way to apply is to mix the thermal protector with your chosen styling product (unless it's a thermal protector spray, in which case it's easier just to spritz it straight on to your hair before you apply the product or use a tool). In addition, there are some new thermal protectors on the market that mix styling benefits along with heat protection. Feel free to give these a try to see how they work for you, but personally, I prefer specific products for specific jobs—if they need to be mixed with other products to get the right effect, no problem.

ADVICE FOR HEAT-TOOL USE

Heat tools like curling and straightening irons are a great addition to your styling arsenal because they allow you to shape and style your hair quickly and easily—a perfect solution to our time-challenged lives, especially since they're so

tips and techniques that can minimize the amount of stress you put on your hair:

When using a curling or straightening iron, take thicker sections of hair into the iron all at once. This means heat is being applied directly to fewer individual hair strands, reducing the amount of heat stress in the process. Take finer sections and you subject your hair to more heat and more stress.

Another great way to diffuse that stress-inducing heat: Keep your heat tools moving as much as possible, no more than fifteen or twenty seconds before moving on to the next section.

Buy irons that have a thermometer gauge and keep your heat tool on the lowest setting possible. Yes, a superhot iron makes your hair straight and smooth right away, but do it a lot and you soon encounter dried-out, frazzled hair that never will be smooth and straight again until you cut off the damage.

Remember, if you use heat tools often, the damage can make it more difficult to achieve a successful color service. That's because the cuticle can become dry and damaged and won't open up as much when color is applied. This means the color fails to lock into the hair shaft as well, reducing the short- and long-term effect of color. If you use a lot of heat tools and you're going in for a color service, be sure to let your stylist know so he or she can compensate for it in the color process.

As a general rule, avoid subjecting your hair to excessive heat whenever possible. A well-executed straight blow out lasts you three days.

And it's likely to look even better on the second or third day because your hair will be less susceptible to frizz and flyaways. So there's no need to blow-dry every day. If you're curling your hair, remember that rollers are a superb way to introduce brilliant, bouncy curls without the heat of a curling iron (see page 213 for more details).

IONIC TECHNOLOGY

Available in brushes, blow dryers, and straightening irons, ionic technology is a powerful hair-styling aid that's been on the market for a few years. Tools with this technology are grabbing a large share of the market, and with good reason—the right ionic tools are even easier and quicker to use than traditional tools; they add shine and strength, reduce static and frizz, and leave your hair feeling soft, smooth, and shiny. Personally I love them, and I'm using ionic tools more and more in my salon.

So how does it work? The answer involves a bit of a science lesson, so bear with me. Ionic technology refers to the creation of negative ions or negatively charged particles. These negative ions are abundant in nature, particularly around water, and are known to have a good natural energy. A few years ago, it was discovered that this energy worked on the hair cuticle. So, very kindly, scientists and innovators found a way to transport these negative ions directly to your hair through tourmaline, a semiprecious crystal and a natural source of ion energy. In short, modern ionic technology in hair care features small amounts of tourmaline crushed and infused into styling tools as a very clever little ion generator.

Although ionic technology is a rapidly growing market, many people are afraid or unwilling to use the technology due to some common misconceptions. First, you can't physically see these ions (although if you look close enough you can see the tourmaline). Because we can't see them, the belief is that they're not actually there and it's a charlatan's trick that doesn't work. This idea is supported by the many cheaper, substandard, ionic tools on the market that don't give the true benefits

of the technology. That leads to the final reason ionic tools are not as commonly used as they might be: the cost. Proper ionic styling tools cost a lot (they do contain a semiprecious crystal, after all), so before you buy, you should know that it's right for you.

Guide to Ionic Technology

Ionic tools cause your hair to become more compact, making the shaft smaller and tighter in diameter (by as much as 25 percent). This is great for chemically treated hair, medium to coarse hair, and curly hair, as it makes your hair shinier, smoother, soft to the touch, and easier to shape, style, and control. Ionic technology also protects color-treated hair from fading. But if you have fine to medium chemically untreated hair, ionic is not generally for you, because ideally you want to puff out the hair shaft for that vital illusion of thickness—the opposite of what ionic does. However, if your hair is fine to medium and your ends are brittle and damaged, then you can use ionic tools just on the ends where this technology helps to repair the stress. This all may sound too good to be true, and I can understand those sentiments, especially if you've never seen or heard of ionic before, but I've been using this technology in my salon for a couple of years now, and I wouldn't recommend it if I didn't feel it was up to the job.

Here's what ionic technology does best:

- Tightens the hair cuticle for shine and smoothness

- Helps prevent fading in chemically treated hair

- Keeps hair soft (traditional heat tools can make hair brittle over time)

- Fights frizz and flyaways

- Speeds drying time

- Protects against the static and frizz induced by heat-humidity

- Helps maintain even levels of moisture throughout the hair shaft

Okay, now let's look at how different ionic tools work, and what features and benefits they have for you.

Ionic brushes. If you're unsure about laying out the money for an ionic dryer or a straightening iron, an ionic brush is a great place to start—you can buy a good one for less than $50. Most common on the market are flat paddle brushes and round bristle brushes. Use them the same way you use any other flat paddle or round bristle brush. How do they work? The brush bristles are infused with tiny tourmaline particles, and, as the brush rotates through your hair, the ions smooth out any roughness in the cuticle, helping you create perfectly groomed, frizz-free looks.

Blow-dryers. In ionic dryers, a tourmaline coating is added to the heat element or nozzle, and, as the hot air flows past the coated area, it carries the ion energy into the hair shaft. This causes the hair cuticle to constrict, in turn reducing the diameter of the hair shaft. A constricted (flatter, straighter, and smoother) cuticle reflects light better for shine; it helps protect against frizz and limp and lifeless hair, as well as the problems resulting from heat-humidity. Ionic dryers also dry your hair more quickly than standard dryers. That's because as your hair is constricted, the water is being squeezed out. These dryers are expensive, thoug—around $200 for a good one.

Straightening irons. Here the tourmaline is crushed into the plates of the straightening iron, which comes into direct contact with your hair. Ionic straightening irons are used in the same way as more traditional tools—again, it's just that they are much more effective at straightening, smoothing, and giving a high-gloss shine to medium-to-thick or chemically treated hair. And, crucially, ionic irons don't cause heat-induced damage. Yes, this is still a hot tool, but the ions really do protect your hair, for the healthiest possible results. These irons range from a 1/2" barrel size up to a 2" barrel size. Just as with other hot irons, smaller barrels are great to get into tight areas, around the ears, nape, and neck, while bigger barrels flat iron bigger sections more quickly. Good ionic straightening irons cost between $100 and $150.

Problem Hair Q & A

In my salon, through snail and e-mail, and even on the street, I get stopped and asked for solutions to styling problems. It's interesting because, mostly, the troubles I hear about cover the same ground. It seems everyone is baffled by frizz, fine or curly hair, and extrathick hair. So I've decided to tackle those typical questions right here, right now. If you encounter a similar problem, my styling solutions will be just the ticket.

My hair is very frizzy, curly, and extremely thick. I want my frizz to be transformed into beautiful shine. Can you give me some tips on what products and styling techniques to use to transform my look and calm my frizz?

Shampoo and condition your hair and towel-dry to damp. Apply a moisture-rich volume-building product like styling crème from the roots to the midsection of your hair shaft. Next, apply a defrizz serum from the midsection through to the ends of your hair shaft. Now execute the wraparound blow-dry technique (page 102) using high heat and a large round brush or a flat paddle brush until your hair is approximately 70 percent or 80 percent dry (more normal types dry through almost completely, that's why on page 101 I recommend drying through 95 percent. Finally, apply a thermal protector product and use a straightening iron to flatten out the roots, paying particular attention to the back of your hair. Take half-inch sections and move through them quickly and easily. Finish with a touch of shine spray, which helps to press your hair flat and adds a brilliant dab of glitz and glamour to your look. You'll have

fabulously sexy, straight, and smoothed-out hair. Alternatively, if you'd like to celebrate your curls, do exactly the same thing, just substitute a large-barrel curling iron for the straightening iron and focus on shaping soft, frizz-free, bouncy curls.

My hair is naturally curly hair that is very fine and thinning. I would like to give the impression of fullness. How do I obtain fullness with my curly hair?

It's easy! Shampoo and condition and then simply execute the controlled curls styling technique (page 113) with the products recommended for fine hair (a volume foam and a curl crème).

My hair is straight, thick, and coarse, and I can't do anything with it. Do you have any tips or techniques I could easily try?

The first thing you need is the right cut. And if your hair is really maddeningly thick, coarse, and straight, you definitely need a shorter style with loads and loads of layers to make your hair easier to manage and control. I recommend the razor-cut graduation cut (page 53) or the cropped razor cut (page 51). Both are the short, manageable styles you need. You can even create magically smooth hair. Just apply the wraparound technique for smoothness as demonstrated on page 102, with one simple change of product. Skip the volume foam and just use lots and lots of defrizz. Your hair doesn't need the added volume, but it definitely does need the smoothing benefits of a serum.

On *What Not to Wear,* I saw you tame an African-American lady's Diana Ross–esque hair. My hair is just like that. Could you please tell me the instructions and products used to do this technique?

This takes time, but it is a highly effective technique for creating shiny controlled curls, just like Diana. Start by applying a moisture-rich, volume-building product like styling crème or curl crème from the roots to the ends of wet to damp hair. Now, from the tips of your hair, grab a one-inch section, pull it taut and straight, then use your fingers to twist it around into a tight spiral. Take the spiraling all the way to your roots and then let it go. Now you can cup this one-inch section in your hands, push it toward your roots, and gently squeeze, squeeze, squeeze for thirty seconds. This locks in your curls, taming any unruly knots or frizz. You can do this in sections all over your head, but I advise focusing on the front and sides and not worrying so much about the back. These areas are much easier for you to work on because you can see what you're doing, and it's where you get the most definition. This look will last you all day. If you want a look to last you all week, use big rollers to reset the formation of your hair into a softer curl texture that you can manipulate into your own shape and style. (Take a look at Chapter 9, "Special-Occasion Hair" for more details.)

Summing It All Up

The biggest lesson you learned from this chapter is that tough-to-manage and troublesome hair have certain limitations in terms of its stylability. But face that reality and apply the right cut, product, or styling technique (and in many cases all three), and getting gorgeous-looking, easy-to-maintain hair should be no trouble at all.

Each type of problem hair has its own simple solution: If you have supercurly hair, get a short and rounded cut that celebrates the shape of your curls and then control those curls with a defrizz serum and a curl-enhancing product. If your hair is sun damaged or overprocessed, protect it from the elements with hats and scarves; repair it with deep-conditioning treatments; and if it gets really bad, simply cut off the damaged hair and let it grow back healthy and sexy. If you have fine to thin hair, get a short haircut that makes your hair look thicker, use light shampoos and conditioners that don't weigh your hair down, and style your hair with a good volumizing product. If you have extrathick hair, go for a short haircut that takes the weight out, or for a long haircut that uses the weight to pull your hair down, straight and flat. If your hair suffers in heat and humidity, work with it in the most natural way. Use moisturizing shampoos and conditioners to put back essential moisture, then use a defrizz serum as your go-to styling product. And for all hair types, problem or not, you can take even more care by using my advice on thermal protectors, ionic technology, and the right way to use heat tools.

Commit to following these guidelines and your problem hair will be a problem no more.

8. My Approach to Ethnic Hair

On an ordinary day working behind the chair in my salon, I noticed, out of the corner of my eye, a beautiful African-American woman. She was tall and slender, with elegant features, great skin, and a fashion-forward outfit. Just one thing was letting her down: her hair. More specifically, her hair extensions. It was a classic case of hair extensions gone bad. They looked tangled and unkempt, and I could see two mismatched textures in her hairstyle—the texture of her natural, kinky Afro trying to get out from underneath the worn-out extensions that weighed down her hair, making her look careless. As she was in the salon waiting for a friend, rather than getting a cut herself, I decided to talk to her between appointments. I told her that I thought she had huge potential but that her extensions were bad, really bad, but if she removed them and worked with her natural ethnic hair instead, she'd look sensational. It took a little bit of convincing, but once she'd taken a long, hard look in the mirror and realized how nasty her extensions had become, she agreed to let me pull them out and give her a much more modern ethnic hairstyle.

The woman is named Arielle, and her transformation from tired, high-maintenance extensions to an easy, fashion-forward style is featured in this chapter. As you'll see, the new hairstyle made a terrific difference in

the way she looked and, as it happens, in the way she felt—because she looked great, she felt fabulous. This natural approach (along with a few other simple ideas) defines my way of tackling ethnic hair, and that's exactly what this chapter is all about.

The Different Ethnic Hair Types

There are two different types of ethnic hair and each requires its own approach. African-American hair grows naturally curly and, crucially, naturally frizzy. It also tends to be very coarse and, apart from the odd exception, the darkest shades of brown. As with any other hair type, there is a rich diversity in the amount of curl, frizz, and coarseness, but African-American women normally have kinky, cottony, spiral-shaped, and woolly hair. Tight curls, thick hair, and heavy density require a unique method to the haircut and to the day-to-day styling.

The second ethnic hair type is most typical of Latina women and women with strong ethnic diversity in their heritage. This hair is normally thick, dense, and curly but it does not form tight, spiral-shaped Afro-type curls. Instead, it looks similar to thick and curly Caucasian hair. Though this hair type can and does benefit from some particular ideas and some particular approaches, it is much more malleable than the Afro, and a lot of the tools and techniques given throughout the rest of this book are also applicable to her.

For that reason, my main focus in this chapter is African-American hair. I do give some special advice for Latina and ethnically diverse hair types later on in this chapter as well, along with some references to other parts of the book that will help you, and a couple of great hairstyles, but I want to start by dealing with the unique challenges presented by beautiful African-American hair.

There are two ways that I recommend women deal with the challenges of this type of hair. The first way, the way that Arielle got a brand-new sense of style, is to work with your natural texture to create an ultrasimple, short classical shape. Simple short and rounded shapes make the hair supereasy to manage and allow you to keep your hair's natural texture while still making the otherwise highly challenging day-to-day styling really simple and easy.

The second way is to use advanced salon techniques to reset the formation of your hair. You can "relax" your hair to make it permanently straight. The biggest benefit of this kind of service is that you have a much wider array of hairstyles and styling options to choose from.

Go for this second option and you can use many of the techniques in Chapter 5, "Styling at Home," to style your hair straight and smooth, or you can roller-set or curling-iron-set your hair into a wavy or curly formation. You may know all about this already, because setting hair has been a popular tradition among ethnic hair types for many years. If you don't know about setting hair, it basically entails using rollers (or for a quicker fix, the curling iron) to set your hair into a different curl formation. For example, if you've relaxed your dense, curly Afro that previously wouldn't budge into a softer, straighter shape, you can now wet your hair, wrap it up on biggish rollers, and allow it to dry. Your hair will be "set" into a softer, more manageable curl formation— bigger, looser curls that you can move and manipulate into a variety of wavy and curly styles, giving you tons more options.

I truly believe that these approaches are the most modern way to style ethnic hair. Most style-savvy African-American women embrace these ideas because they transform their look into something contemporary, cool, and easy to manage and care for. Let's start with hair relaxing, a technique that features heavily in the haircuts in this chapter.

Relaxers

Relaxers are a great way to work fresh, young, and modern. They can straighten your hair completely or, by using less chemical strength, give you a softer, more manageable, wavy or curly style. Both ways increase your options in terms of haircuts you can go for, and, of course, you can roller-set your hair any way you wish. But keep in mind that this process permanently alters the composition of your hair both in terms of its shape (into a straighter or softer curl than is natural) and also its health (hair normally becomes drier than normal). For a relaxer, the most common active chemical ingredient is sodium hydroxide. The chemical process is a

strong one and breaks the structure of your hair bonds into a new straighter shape. For many African-American women, the big question is whether or not to relax the hair. With such a strong chemical process, damage is a risk, and immediately after the treatment, drier, less healthy hair is a virtual certainty (at least until you've helped it out with some deep conditioning and/or keratin-based treatments). Another factor is whether you truly want to permanently change the traditional texture of your hair. On the bright side, you will get much more variety in the way you can cut and style your hair, with the day-to-day styling made considerably more manageable. And if you don't relax or treat the hair in any way, you are very limited in what you can do with your hair. To aid you in that decision, let's examine what this modern salon professional treatment means for you. Then you can take a look at the ethnic hairstyles below, where many of the styles have been relaxed.

The process of relaxing smoothes and flattens the hair into a much straighter shape and style, or totally straight if you use enough strength. Relaxers have improved over the years so that they no longer make the hair ultradry and brittle—yes, it is drier than before the treatment, but it shouldn't be too serious. Because of this, it is becoming an increasingly popular salon service. It's a safe process for most hair types and it improves your hair's feel, softness, and shine, leaving it completely manageable. More and more of my African-American clients are interested in this technique and frequently ask what it can and can't do, how safe it is, and

many more questions pertaining to the technique. The best way to get to the bottom of it all is to give you a Q & A session of everything that is important to you.

Relaxer Q & A

How much does relaxing cost?

Relaxing your hair is a time-consuming specialty process. It takes from two to three hours, and during that time your stylist should be totally consumed with processing your hair. But the results save you many hours of blow-dry styling. Because of all that, expect to pay anywhere from $75 to $200, depending on how strongly you relax your hair (the more you relax, the more it costs) and on your location and your stylist's experience as a relaxer specialist. However, almost everybody who goes for this treatment ends up happy with the results and considers it a great investment. Retouch treatments require just as much time and just as much skill, so the price is the same.

How do relaxers work?

A good relaxer stylist gives your hair a deep-conditioning treatment to add strength and vitality along with a "relaxer" that safely and effectively re-forms the structural bonds within the hair shaft. This re-formation allows the hair's curl or frizz patterns to be restructured into a totally straight look. Once these structural

bonds are relaxed, the stylist uses heat to permanently fix this new straightened structure into place.

Chemicals cause damage in the hair shaft. Will a relaxer cause damage to my hair?

If you go to an experienced professional, you'll get a thorough consultation to determine if your hair is in suitable condition for a relaxing process. If your hair is healthy, there should be no problems. On the other hand, if your hair is fine, weak, or overprocessed, there is a risk of breakage and a good stylist will recommend a course of deep conditioning and/or protein-rich, keratin-based treatments to toughen up your hair before having it relaxed. A relaxer does need the right aftercare, but nowadays the process is designed to leave hair soft and manageable.

Will my curls come back?

After a relaxer treatment, your hair can be restored to its original texture only by allowing it to grow back in. You can, of course, style your newly straightened hair into dozens of different styles. For example, if you want to create some waves and curls, you can use the creating curl technique on page 114 or the curling irons technique on page 116. Alternatively, you can roller-set your hair for more long-lasting waves and curls, as outlined later in this chapter and in Chapter 9, "Special Occasion Hair." However, once done, the process cannot be reversed to restore the original texture to treated hair.

Is there anything I need to do prior to my treatment in order to prepare my hair the right way?

Before you go in for a relaxing treatment, you could, over the course of two or three weeks, apply a deep conditioner or keratin-based

> **B**efore you go in for a relaxing treatment, you could . . . apply a deep conditioner or keratin-based treatment several times.

treatment several times to put extra moisture and protein into your hair. However, most important, do not shampoo or condition your hair for at least forty-eight hours prior to your appointment. If you do, irritation of the scalp is a real possibility. If you don't shampoo for forty-eight hours before, there should be nothing to worry about. If you have any concerns, speak to your stylist.

What is the relaxing aftercare process?

It's imperative that you keep your hair dry for seventy-two hours after the process. This gives the restructured hair shafts time to harden and set into their new formation. Also, it's a good idea to keep your hair as straight as possible during this time to avoid any kinks. Don't tie your hair back with clips, grips, or bands.

Tucking your hair behind your ears is another no-no. After seventy-two hours, and assuming there has been no irregular damage (your stylist will tell you what to do in the unlikely event that there has been), you can shampoo, dry, and style your hair any way you want, although the less heat you use, the better you maintain the health and integrity of your new style.

How long will my relaxer treatment last?

Relaxing permanently straightens your hair. Once the relaxed hair grows out, typically around four to six weeks, you want to go back to the salon for a retouch. This is important, because if you don't get the retouch, you end up with mismatched hair texture: your natural curls growing in at the roots versus your straighter relaxed texture throughout the rest of the hair. The retouch is quite a tricky process and I strongly advise going back to the same stylist who relaxed your hair in the first place to ensure the consistency of the result.

Can I color my hair with a relaxing treatment?

Yes. It is best to have your hair color done after the relaxing, because a relaxer is likely to cause fading and damage to prior color. You should wait for at least a week after the relaxer until your coloring.

The extra styling freedom you get from a

relaxer also gives your stylist more freedom. If you get a haircut after one of these processes, your stylist has a wider range of styles to offer you. Let's look at that right now, with the help of my ethnic hairstyle guide.

The Hairstyles

For me, the key factor in a great African-American hairstyle is keeping it simple. For the hairdresser, it's a visual and technical type of haircut where he or she is working slowly, surely, and carefully to create the shape. Again, a great hairdresser is vital, and I encourage you to follow the guidelines set forth in Chapter 4, "Finding a Hairdresser," to make sure you've got the right hairdresser for you. Whether you decide to go short, medium, or long, keep the style easy and uncomplicated. Otherwise, as your hair grows out and the curls grow in, even with a relaxer, the details of the cut become unkempt and look unnatural. By keeping it simple, you also can go home and use tools like hot irons and rollers to change and define your style from day to day and week to week, according to your mood, inclination, and available time. Once ethnic hair has been cut correctly and prepped to be healthy, smooth, and moisture rich, you can easily use tools to create different shapes, waves, and curl movements, just as I explain in Chapter 5, "Styling at Home."

Let's get you started. The cuts here show a variety of ways that you can wear your relaxed Afro hair. I explain the benefits of each cut and some of the individual styling options.

KIM

Kim is a busy mom with a big family, and she needed her wonderfully curly but tough-to-control Afro hair to be supereasy. With her hectic schedule, it was critical to make her hair manageable. We gave her a relatively gentle relaxer treatment to soften out her heavy curl action and add more *give* in hair that was originally almost unmovable and difficult even to get a brush or product to go through. The softer curls enabled us to scissor-cut her hair in a soft and round style that falls beautifully around her warm, engaging face. And it's still curly, showcasing the traditional texture of her hair, but in a smooth and elegant way. I thought Kim's natural hair color was a perfect fit for her looks. If it ain't broke, don't fix it. We left it natural.

This is the *ultimate* ethnic wash-and-wear style. It doesn't need to be touched or towel dried at all, and if you go for a similar style, all you need to do is apply a very small amount of a curl enhancer and an even smaller amount of a frizz-fighting serum. Let it dry naturally and you're off. A modern, soft, and natural look with absolutely no fuss.

NATALIE

Natalie had curly Afro hair that was also comparatively fine in texture. We gave her a relaxer that added essential silky smoothness, followed by a light brown highlight to soften the complexion of her hair, bring out the beauty in her eyes, and give her an allover bubbly glow. After that, she was ready for a brand-new, style-defining look—a textured layer cut with the layers shaped to fall loosely around her face, acting as the perfect complement to her features.

This is an ultramodern way of wearing ethnic hair because the relaxer option makes it possible to cut in a contemporary hairstyle that works with all hair types. The true beauty of the style is that you can wear your hair in many different ways; without the relaxer, I would have had to go for a more rounded short and curly shape.

Now Natalie has a modern style and the opportunity to wear it in new ways. A defrizz serum and a straightening iron create a supersmooth and polished straight look. Or, as here, you can use a defrizz serum with a round brush to give the style more wave and movement, body and bounce. You can also use a curling iron to tousle the tresses more.

KASHA

A relaxer straightened and smoothed out Kasha's kinky, dried-out, and way out-of-control Afro. We added some light brown-sugar tones to provide warmth and to soften the picture of her hair. That allowed us to cut her hair with our options completely open. We got creative and gave her a fresh and new above-the-shoulder square layer cut that stands out—it's flirty, choppy, and modern look. It definitely illuminates her gorgeous, happy features.

It's the versatility Kasha now has that makes this a truly great cut. Before the process of change, it was a challenge for her to get to the office on time without her hair looking unkempt and unprofessional, all because she had a dried-out, thick, and curly Afro. Now she can use a flat brush and a touch of defrizz serum to quickly blow-dry her hair straight and smooth for daily office wear. Or, because of the layers, she can use a curling iron to add fabulous flippiness, just like we've done here.

If you go for a similar style and want to use a curling iron, you don't need a styling product. A thermal protector to protect the hair does the trick, and you can use your hot tool on dry hair to add some light twists and twirls for the striking, featherweight effect you see here.

ARIELLE

Arielle is the charming, beautiful woman I talked about in my introduction to this chapter. She is a classic case of hair extensions gone bad. The before pictures clearly show that the two textures—that of her natural hair and that of her extensions—simply don't match. The extensions also look frazzled and were becoming a tangled nightmare for her to try to style. Thankfully, Arielle was game for a change and was happy to have me cut out the extensions so I could work with her natural hair texture. You can see she has a long, slender, and elegant neck, so I cut her hair into a simple, classic rounded shape that highlights this feature and adds elevation for her facial features. Her hair looks supershort, but actually it's rather long; it's just so tight and curly you can't see the length. The cut makes her look young and hip, which is exactly what she is, a vast improvement on the extensions that looked shabby and failed to showcase her beaming smile.

It's a hassle-free, wash-and-wear cut, too. All she has to do is apply a setting crème or lotion to help the hair hold its shape and a defrizz product to keep it smooth. There's no need for brushing or touching.

ELSY

Elsy also had a tough-to-control, I-need-all-your-attention Afro that we relaxed to make the hair nice and smooth, with a healthy glow. We

gave her a classic long layer cut that has space and movement, swing, body, and bounce. We also put in a fresh new color, in this case a demipermanent dark chocolate brown that fits with her complexion and gives added sheen and luster to her hair.

This style also offers quick-and-easy styling options that make it ever so wearable from day to day and easily transformable for a night out and about. Here, too, there's no need for too much product, which only weighs down ethnic hair. The tiniest dab of a frizz-fighting serum used with a flat brush and the heat of a dryer creates a silky smooth look that's sure to get you noticed. As an alternative, and/or if you want some extra luster before you head out, use a straightening iron to add sheen and polish to any sort of straight style. You can try this on dry hair with no product application. Just a quick spritz or two of shine spray gives it that glistening finish. For a few flirty waves or curls, use a curling iron instead. Work it through a few sections and you're good to go.

That's how I like to work with relaxed Afro hair. You can see that it gives you lots more options for all kinds of modern, fashion-forward, and easy-to-manage hairstyles. However, in many cases, I like to work with Afro hair in a more natural way, to celebrate a woman's natural curliness. These types of hairstyles are more limited, but if you get the right kind of natural cut, you can still go for a modern, fashion-forward, and easy-to-manage hairstyle.

Styling and Setting Ethnic Hair

If, like Arielle, you can wear your Afro hair relatively short and naturally curly with individuality and style, then great, I certainly encourage you to do so. Follow the simple advice I gave in her haircut descriptions and you'll be fine. You don't need too much product because that only weighs your hair down, while touching and playing with it too much creates frizz. If your curly style is a bit dried out, apply a leave-in conditioner to rejuvenate the hair by bringing the moisture back. Want to hold it in place? A little bit of setting lotion or crème is all you need. Work it through from roots to ends and your style will stay put. If frizz is a problem, you know what to do: A dab of defrizz serum is all you need.

However, if a thick and curly Afro style didn't work for you, and you've gone for a relaxer and now want to shape your own waves and curls rather than styling it straight all the time, roller-setting is your next port of call.

The technique I recommend for you is called the roller "wet set" because this is the longest-lasting type of set and allows you to wear your set all week long without it needing to be redone. I take a lot of time to describe roller-setting (the wet set and other great setting techniques) on page 218, because setting your hair is great for all hair types, Caucasian and ethnic, to achieve a magical special-occasion hairstyle. But setting hair does have a deeper meaning for ethnic hair types because, as I've discussed, some Afro hair can be unmanageable unless tended to. So, for many, this roller-setting is more of a week-to-week essential than a special-occasion do. That's why you see a lot of African-American women in the salon from week to week: They're getting their relaxed hair reset into a curl formation that will last them all week long and can be easily blown out and styled as they see fit.

The wet set sets your hair into more manageable curls. When you leave your hair to dry on rollers, you can reset it into a wider, easier-to-control-and-manipulate curly hairstyle. You need relatively large sponge rollers to produce open, loose curls and create movement. If you can fit only eight to ten rollers in your hair, you know they are big enough.

THE WET SET

1. On wet hair, cleanly comb each section of hair before working with the rollers. This helps ensure that your curls are tangle free and won't snag and snarl up in the roller. Use a wide-tooth comb to comb through your hair until it's free from knots.

2. Now that your hair is free of tangles, apply a setting spray, lotion, or crème all over the hair, paying particular attention to the roots. Use soft-hold products if you envision a soft, flowing look. Use firmer-hold products if you want a more sculptured style. Though it's not a typical wet-set product, I also advise you work in just a touch of defrizz serum. This doesn't affect the setting of your hair, but it helps fight against the frizz common to ethnic hair.

3. Now it's time to put in the rollers. Sit in front of a mirror so you can see exactly what you're doing. Don't worry too much about the precise placement of the rollers, just be careful that you get a nice even spread across the front, top, sides, and back. Do this and your look is sure to be well balanced.

4. Part a section of hair that is the same width as your roller, no wider, and give that section another quick comb through to make sure there are no snags. Why do I emphasize that the width of the section of the hair you have parted away be the same width as the roller and no wider? Because pulling hair from outside the width of the roller creates drag. This stops the roller from sitting securely on your head and you end up with less consistent, floppy waves and curls that fail to last.

5. Now that your hair is parted correctly, take that section and pull it up and away from the scalp with your thumb and fingertips. Make sure the hair is taut with no creases or loose bits and hold it in position as close to the tips of your hair as you can without letting any of it fall free. If your hair has an uneven line at the ends, no problem; unless you've had a real hack job, the difference will be negligible and have little or no effect on how the hair sits, and subsequently sets, in the rollers.

6. Hold your hair in place while you use your free hand to place the roller as close to the tips of the hair shaft as you can. Wrap the roller around the hair gently and smoothly, making sure that it catches and holds onto the hair. Now place both of your thumbs over the ends of the roller and roll the hair firmly down toward the scalp.

7. Once done, clip the rollers firmly into place to make sure they stay put. Repeat these steps with six to eight biggish rollers placed evenly over your head.

8. After completing the rollers, apply another liberal amount of setting spray all over your hair, with particular emphasis on the roots of the rolled sections. Note: You need a spray here because you can't get a foam or crème to reach your roots while the rollers are in place.

9. Let your hair dry naturally, overnight, if you can (but you have to use soft sponge rollers if you are planning to sleep with them in). This ensures that you create a striking difference to your natural curl formation—and a striking difference that lasts up to a week.

10. Unroll and unwind the rollers the same way you put them in—gently and smoothly. Resist any temptation to speed the process by dragging them out—this definitely destroys your style.

Short and Curly

If you have short hair (in a similar style to Arielle's) that hasn't been relaxed, making your hair straight and smooth is still achievable. Use the wraparound blow-dry technique highlighted on page 102. Instead of using a brush, however, use a fine-tooth comb, which is a great tool for getting into the roots and tousling them out. Get right into those roots and use the heat of the dryer, a defrizz serum, and a smoothing crème or lotion to achieve gorgeously smooth, short hair. If at the end it's still a bit curly, wavy, or kinky, use a straightening iron to smooth out and straighten even more. Bear in mind, however, that this technique doesn't have the potential to last all week like a wet set does; it lasts only about a day.

11. Remember, no hairstyle is truly set until it's cool, so give your hair a quick blast of cool air with your dryer. If the style you've created is more curly than you envisioned, no problem. Your hair is still malleable, so use a blow-dryer and a brush to brush out the curl until you've got the look you want.

12. With a wet set, the slower setting time can leave set lines on your hair, at exactly the place where the rollers were placed, creating a darker band of color running across your hair. There is a quick and easy fix for this: Brush them out.

13. Finally, brush and shape your hair into your desired style, and be sure to make yourself look stunning. Now you can fix the look into place with hair spray or holding spray.

14. If you wish, you can use a straightening or curling iron on the ends to create a custom-made finish to your look. Simply curl or twist up a few loose ends around the front and sides to add your own individual polished elegance. Refine the style with an iron once it's set, rather than trying to create all the shape and texture at once.

Done correctly, the wet set is a great method of getting your hair to hold its new shape and texture for up to a week. All you need to do is give it a quick one-minute blast with a blow-dryer and brush each morning to refresh and redefine your style. Steer clear of using too much product, though, because that increases the dirt, and as you won't be washing your hair until the next time you set it, you want to avoid dirt as much as possible. Apply a dab of defrizz if you're worried it might frizz up; otherwise, the natural sebum oils of your scalp give you enough texture to play with and create luscious everyday style.

THE CURLING IRON SET

If you'd like your straightened hair to have a loose and natural-looking wave or curl pattern but the wet set is too much work, use a curling iron instead. Though it isn't as long lasting as a wet roller-set (a curling iron set normally lasts twenty-four hours at the most), a curling iron creates almost exactly the same effect. It's easy, too.

Mist in a thermal protecting spray and put sections of your hair into the curling iron. Then curl, twist, and shape your personal wave or curl pattern to your heart's content. Start at the front, where it's easiest to do, and then move on to sections across the top, sides, and back. Make sure to hold the iron in each section long enough for it to stay set. This normally takes around thirty seconds per section. If you want more information on how to best use a curling iron, look at "Curling Irons" on page 116 and "The Curling Iron Set" on page 226.

Other Options

If you find working with your natural hair limiting and are not into the idea of permanently resetting the texture of your hair with a relaxer, there are some other options open to you. Extensions, weaves, or even clip-on hairpieces instantly give you different length and texture, even different colors. You can go to your local beauty supply store and shop for new hairpieces that provide dramatic, temporary results with little or no damage done.

One of the most popular ways to go is to add length (and/or a new color) with a weft or weave. A weft features loose strands of hair—either natural or synthetic, though most are synthetic—that, through braiding techniques, can be combined with your natural hair (whatever the length) to add length or color or both to your look.

In a weave, a separate hairpiece is sewn or glued along a "track" to add length and/or color. The track is like a hem of hair, sewn tight together on one end (like an anchor), which allows the hair to flow freely, very much like natural hair. Then the actual track is either glued or sewn into a cornrow and then carefully hidden by the section of hair that falls above it.

Glued-in tracks last only a week or two at the most, whereas braided-in tracks can last between three and six weeks, depending on the quality of the hairpiece and the quality of the application.

Wefts generally are synthetic, but weaves come in both natural and synthetic hairpieces. The difference? Synthetic pieces have a shorter life span and cannot be washed or conditioned, nor can they be styled with hot tools—they're plastic and will melt. On the other hand, natural hairpieces can be washed and conditioned just like your own hair and can be styled with the aid of hot tools and blow-dryers.

These techniques can be done at home, with the wefts and weaves costing anywhere from $15 to $100. However, you should check the packet to see how much hair you're getting, because if you're planning to use a lot you may need more than one pack.

If this all sounds like a lot of work, but you would still like to try something of this ilk, a great way to go is a clip-in extension. This is available

> Synthetic pieces have a shorter life span and cannot be washed or conditioned, nor can they be styled with hot tools.

from your beauty supply store and is relatively cheap, between $5 and $50 depending on how elaborate it is. Clip-ins work great when you want a clip-in ponytail or if you need an extra piece of hair to style into an updo. And because it's a clip, there's no sewing or gluing.

Want to go to a professional? There are specialty salons that do an excellent job. Again, I recommend revisiting Chapter 4, "Finding a Hairdresser," and applying those same rules to finding the right person for these specialty techniques. Depending on how much and how detailed the work you want to have done, the cost can range from $60 to $400. I advise that the professional way is the best choice for this kind of specialty ethnic hair processes,

especially if you are considering a weave. It's not easy to create a seamless transition from your natural hair to the added-in extensions, and a professional should be able to create the look you desire without an obvious contrast between the two different textures. Professional extensions are likely to last longer, too. Keep in mind that in addition to the service cost ($60–$400), you have to pay for the extra hair. Depending on the quality of the weaves/wefts you buy, this may cause a significant markup. Natural hair, although more expensive, always looks better than synthetic hair. With natural hair extensions you need have no fear of thermal styling. In my opinion, if you're investing in this type of service, you may as well go the extra mile and get the best hairpiece possible.

Hispanic and Ethnically Diverse Hair Types

If you have thick and curly non-Afro ethnic hair, there's a lot more room for you to work successfully with your natural hair shape and texture. Your thick, dense curls can still be tough to manage and style if you don't treat them the right way, though, so if you want to work with your natural texture and shape, the first thing you must do is get the right type of haircut. You need a heavily layered cut that creates enough space between the curls to free the hair from tangles and celebrate the unique shapeliness of your textured tresses. The big bonus of this approach is that you can keep your hair's natural texture but still make the otherwise highly challenging day-to-day styling really simple and easy. Indeed, cut the right way, this type of hair benefits from many of the easy curly-hair styling techniques illustrated in Chapter 5, "Styling at Home." I also show off some salon secrets that are the perfect solution for really thick and dense curly heads of all races. Both of those sections will be a great help to you, especially if you begin with a great haircut. Also, don't forget that these types of curls are loose and malleable enough to be set with rollers or with a curling iron.

Setting your hair with rollers or an iron puts you in control of just how strong or soft, wavy or curly your hair is. This may be something you want to do from day to day, week to week, or maybe just for a special occasion. It is a great option for changing or personalizing your style. See page 197 for the wet roller-set and Chapter 9, "Special-Occasion Hair," for special-occasion styling techniques.

Though roller-setting definitely is a great option for change and for personalized style, with the right cut your day-to-day styling is super-supersimple. You don't need any blow-drying, and just a little product application followed by cupping, scrunching, and tousling out your curls are more than enough to get you, and your curls, looking flame-hot. To see just how easy it is to do that, I'll show you two fabulous curl-defining cuts that truly celebrate naturally curly ethnic hair.

TASHNA

Tashna has a natural curly hair type with heavy density. However, the relatively medium-smooth texture means that we can work with her natural style. I gave her a rounded bob shape, cut with space and freedom, that plays into her charismatic, youthful exuberance and drapes ever so slightly into her sparkle-happy blue-brown eyes, making them pop. The light brown caramel highlights show the texture and dimension of her curl formation. Again, because I worked with her hair in a modern and natural way, she now has the space and freedom that make styling easy.

There's no need to blow-dry; in fact there's barely any need to touch the hair at all. All she needs to do is use product to shape and define her look. If you don't add moisture, this hair type is prone to frizz, so Tashna needs to apply a leave-in conditioner on damp hair to lock in the moisture and shine. She can then use a frizz fighter. Finally, all Tashna needs to do is twist a few curls in the front sections around her fingers to create nicely defined spiral shapes that enhance the beauty of the cut and the beauty of the girl. She can leave the rest of the hair alone to set into its natural shape. If the curls clump together a bit too tightly, just use the fingers to tousle them out—easy. If a touch more hold and shine is needed to add dazzle, or just to make it last, then use a spritz or two of a light-hold hair spray.

ERIKA

Erika has thick, dense, and curly hair. She's a beautiful young woman, but before she came to me, her hair was so thick and long with no true

shape that her old-fashioned, frumpy hairstyle was weighing her down. She also complained about how difficult it was for her to manage her hair from day to day. If you don't get the right type of cut, this hair texture becomes tangled and tough to control. I left her hair relatively long but scissor-cut it with lots and lots of layers to give her hair softness, with enough space to allow us to see the features of her face. I also used the undercutting technique, giving beautiful definition and separation to her curls. This extra space is critical because Erika's hair is now tangle free, making styling so much easier. The look was finished with gorgeous caramel highlights that perfectly suit her complexion and frame the layers of the cut and the features of her face.

Erika's is very much a wash-and-wear style. She doesn't need to blow-dry or brush it at all because that only induces frizz. If you go for a similar style, drying with a diffuser gives you extra volume but, to me, the best way to style it is to let it dry naturally. All you have to do is scrunch in a styling crème, foam, or lotion for lovely fullness and volume and then a curl-enhancing product to set the formation of your curls. Finish by having fun gently twisting a few curls with your fingers for added definition. You'll look stunning. With this hair length, pulling the hair back into a pony or twist is another great option. I love natural curls that are pulled back; they always look so shapely and so sexy.

(Of course, both of these styles also suit the roller-setting techniques I mentioned previously.)

Your Go-To Styling Products

- If you have thick, heavy, curly, or Afro hair, too much of *any* product only weighs down your hair, so remember to use only a bit.

- Frizz is the biggest concern for ethnic hair types because the hair tends to be naturally dry and curly, so your number one product is an antifrizz serum.

- A curl-enhancing product is also a great help when you're wearing curls. Curl enhancers add shape and definition to already curly hair, and you need only a dab or two to get bouncy and voluptuous curls.

- A leave-in conditioner is another terrific product if you wear your hair naturally curly. The moisture-giving benefits fight the frizz while also giving you a touch more shine.

- If you roller-set your hair, you need a setting lotion, crème, or gel to hold the set in place. Once again, look for good-quality products that are oil- or moisture-based for maximum performance.

- Finally, you may want one or more finishing products like a hair or holding spray and a shine enhancer. The hair or holding spray gives you longer-lasting hold; a shine product adds dazzle, glamour, and glitz to any finished do.

Hair Still Too Tough to Manage? Try Thermal Reconditioning

As I've said, hair is as unique as a fingerprint. For women who have thick, dense, and curly Hispanic or ethnically diverse hair, perhaps with some frizz, too, day-to-day styling can be a tough challenge, even with a great haircut. If this rings true for you, an innovative new technique presses frizzy, curly, or wavy hair flat and straight. Thermal reconditioning was invented in Japan to re-form Japanese women's typically thick and tough-to-manage hair into straighter, smoother, and shinier shapes and textures that are soft and easy to style. To give you the tools to find out whether this would be a good option for you, let's tackle some of the most common client questions.

Thermal Reconditioning Q & A

How long does a thermal reconditioning treatment last?

Whatever hair gets treated remains permanently straight. It never becomes curly or wavy again. The new growth that appears in the months following the treatment needs to be thermally reconditioned to match the texture in the rest of your hair. This new growth usually needs to be treated about four to six months after the initial process.

What kind of hair is suitable for thermal reconditioning?

Thermal reconditioning works well for most hair types except African-American Afro types. Afro hair is too fragile and cannot withstand the excessive heat. Latin, Asian, and Middle Eastern hair types are all great for this treatment, as are Caucasian and European hair.

What will my hair look like afterward?

Your hair will be straight and will feel genuinely soft and silky, with more shine.

Will I need to blow-dry my hair after the treatment?

If you want to blow-dry to obtain a particular style, you can certainly do it, no problem.

However, just quickly blasting with heat for two minutes to get the moisture out should be all you need. Add some product, use your fingers to style, and you are ready to rock.

When I get the new growth retreated, will my stylist thermally recondition my whole head all over again?

No, just the new growth is treated. The previously treated hair is usually protected by using oil or conditioner so the solution doesn't work its way into it. If there is still curl or wave in the previously treated hair, solution can be applied, but for a shorter period of time. Note: The retouch is often more difficult to perform. I recommend that you go back to the same stylist who successfully treated you in the first place.

I have color in my hair. Does that matter?

Tints and semipermanent hair color that *deposit* color are not usually any problem at all. Highlights are more tricky to work with. When hair is highlighted, usually bleach is involved. This makes the timing very difficult because some hair is lightened right next to hair that is not lightened. The hair may process fast where highlights are present and need much more time where the hair is dark and unprocessed. A prior consultation with your stylist is necessary to determine if thermal reconditioning is possible for those with highlighted hair. Bleached hair is not suitable for thermal reconditioning.

Will I get any breakage as a result of a bad treatment?

It is possible. If the stylist is inexperienced, you could get breakage from the service, although this almost never occurs with a trained and competent specialist. Be sure to find out how many treatments your stylist has performed and how long he or she has been doing it. You don't want to be a guinea pig while your stylist is still training.

How much does thermal reconditioning cost?

Typically from $300 to $1,000, depending upon the length of the hair, its thickness, the amount of previous chemical processing and, of course, the stylist's experience. It costs a lot because it takes a long time to do, normally between three and six hours, and it is a difficult treatment to perform, making it a real specialists' field.

Healthy Ethnic Hair

Although for styles and styling there are definite differences depending on the type of ethnic hair you have, keeping your hair healthy requires the same basic approach.

Ethnic hair is most commonly porous and dry, hence the frizz. This hair type loses moisture easily and because of that you need to invest a bit of extra time to make sure it stays healthy, soft, and manageable. This is especially true if you plan to have any salon straightening procedures, because to be successful your hair must first be in tip-top shape. The bottom line: Adding moisture is essential for you.

The first thing to do is to make sure you are using the right shampoo and conditioner and then supplement them with weekly or monthly treatments that give your hair added moisture support. Whereas Caucasian hair normally (unless it's unusually dry and frizzy or heavily processed) becomes oversaturated, limp, and lifeless with the use of oil-based and moisture-rich products, ethnic hair needs shampoos and conditioners that are rich in oil and moisture. Even as far back as three thousand years ago, Egyptian women used oils as part of their own hair care regimen, and today you should walk like an Egyptian to tame your own curly, frizzy hair. Oil- and moisture-based shampoos and conditioners literally provide a sealed barrier that holds in the hair's moisture. Even better, look for products especially formulated for ethnic hair types. One warning: Don't fall into the trap of believing that just because the bottle says it is specially designed for your hair, it's a quality product. The best way to know for sure what you're getting is to check the ingredients list. Look for coconut or nut oil, both great natural ingredients in shampoos and conditioners for helping to maintain the integrity of your hair. Also see if the product contains panthenol (or vitamin B_5), a great ingredient to add moisture and shine. If not, what other moisture-giving ingredients does it contain? Look at the label to see if it makes a moisture-giving promise. You want the packaging and/or the person selling you the product to make clear that the product contains the right oils and the right moisture for your hair.

Just like with thick, unmanageable Caucasian hair types, I recommend you condition your hair more often than you shampoo. Remember, shampoo keeps the scalp clean and stops the natural oils that build up on your scalp from working their way through your hair. Obviously you don't want dirty or smelly hair, but a few days of natural oils working through your locks add nice texture and help you to shape and style your look. Conditioner, on the other hand, is an everyday essential. It keeps your hair soft and malleable, and you definitely do want that.

A weekly deep-conditioning treatment penetrates the hair shaft for lasting moisture support. As an alternative (or in addition if your hair needs lots of moisture), a monthly keratin-based, protein-filled treatment adds strength, which reduces the risk of breakage. This is particularly important if you use a lot of heat tools or are preparing for a salon straightening or retexturizing treatment. These products should be available in your beauty supply store or drugstore, but, don't forget, if you go to your salon to pick them up, you'll be able to double-check with a professional about which one is right for you.

Summing It All Up

Ethnic hair is some of the most challenging to work with, and my approach is to simplify cutting and styling as much as possible. First of all, it's important to recognize the two different ethnic hair types: African-American hair is typically curly and frizzy and coarse; Hispanic and ethnically diverse hair is typically thick and dense and curly. Each requires a tailor-made approach.

For African-American hair, I like to work with the natural texture to create short and simple shapes that are modern and easy to manage. Or I like to relax the hair, resetting the curl formation so that there are more possibilities to work with. This second option lets you style your hair straight and smooth or shape your own curly hairstyle with the roller-setting technique. Both approaches make many of the styling options talked about in the rest of the book, and especially Chapter 5, "Styling at Home," completely achievable. Both ways make day-to-day styling easier for you; they're both fashion-forward and sure to give you a style you'll love.

Hispanic and ethnically diverse ethnic hair has its own challenges, too, but it is more malleable than African-American hair, and by following a few guidelines you'll also find that most of the techniques discussed throughout the book are achievable. For you, heavily layered haircuts that break up the density in your hair and celebrate your natural curl formation require only simple day-to-day styling. Use moisture-based styling products and a touch of frizz-fighting serum, and your hair truly is wash-and-wear—and looks fabulous, too. If your hair is *so* thick and dense that even the most heavily layered cuts still leave it difficult to control, you can explore thermal reconditioning—a great way to soften your curly hair texture.

9. Special-Occasion Hair

You now know everything you need for getting Great Hair every day. But what about those special days when you truly want to feel extraordinary? It's time to learn how to change the natural shape and style of your hair to create dos that "Wow!" Wouldn't it be nice, if you have totally straight hair, to be able to create a romantic look with bountiful, flowing waves? Wouldn't it be nice, if you have naturally curly hair, to be able to smooth it out into a softer, more polished look? And wouldn't it be nice to have the skills, the know-how, and the confidence to create simple, classic updos? Well, that's exactly what this chapter is going to teach you!

Making these kinds of changes to your natural shape and style is only slightly more difficult than your everyday hairstyling, and the final results are certainly worth the extra time and effort. Yes, these techniques are a bit more time-consuming and, for the first trial or two, a bit trickier, but my purpose is still the same: to offer you *simple* styling techniques that empower you to make big changes in the way you look. For special occasions, or even if you just like to change things up from time to time (and I'm all for that), you want something different from your normal, everyday style. The techniques I detail in this chapter are the easiest ones to give the kind of dramatic change in your look that will turn heads. I'll give you the lowdown on the quickest and most effective ways to alter or enhance your hair's natural tendencies, so that, with just a touch of practice, you have the freedom to create looks that blow you—and your friends—away.

The trick to pulling off big transformations is the age-old art of setting hair. You can use rollers, pins, and hot tools to reset the natural shape of your hair to build a foundation that allows you to easily create a different look and a different you—perfect for any type of special occasion, perfect for any time you want to give yourself a revitalizing lift, and perfect to have a *lot* of fun with. As you'll see, some of these techniques can be long-lasting, too, so if you discover a set and style you love, by doing it right you'll be able to wear it like that all week long with just a five-minute blast of your blow-dryer each morning. Who doesn't like the sound of that?

In this final chapter, I want you to take all your newfound hairstyling knowledge and use it to experiment with different ways to shape and style your look. Find out what you can create, and have fun doing it! Remember that change and reinvention are good and that your hair is a big part of achieving those things for yourself. Don't think of your hair as a fixed part of your look that can never change. Sure, you want to look great quickly and easily from day to day, but you also want the ability to change your look and make yourself that much more striking. My message for this chapter is this: Learn how to set your hair in a variety of ways, understand that it's your foundation to begin creating new looks, and then simply have fun creating!

Because some of these techniques can be a bit tricky, I encourage you to test them before going out on the town. If fact, if you are having a night in with the girls, why not turn it into a hair party? Styling each other's hair over a bottle or two of bubbly is a great way to practice the techniques. *And* it's sure to capture the imagination of all your friends!

Why Set Your Hair

Practically anyone can benefit from setting her hair. The critical factor in changing your normal hairstyle into something special is getting the preparation right. The reason: On average, you have around 100,000 hairs on your head, so when you want to change your hair's natural look, you have to get all those individual hair strands together and unified for the cause. Do that and your hair instantly becomes easier to manipulate into different shapes and styles, curls and waves. Even though you are changing the natural shape of your hair, your aim is still to work *with* your hair rather than against it.

The best way to get your hair ready for a new look is to set it. And the easiest, most effective way to set your hair is the same way my mom has been setting her own hair for the past forty years—with rollers. A breeze to work with, rollers get all your hairs working together so you can shape and style in a new way without your hair falling back into its natural state as soon as you walk out the door. Because rollers come in different forms, shapes, and sizes, you can change your style radically or make a small, subtle change. It all depends on how you want to look.

SIZES OF ROLLERS

A trip to your local beauty supply shop may leave you feeling confused. What should you buy? That depends. The first thing to consider is which size rollers are right for you.

Rollers generally come in several sizes, from petite (usually about 5/8" diameter) to jumbo (usually about 1½" diameter). The size you should buy depends on two things: the length of your hair and the type of effect you're going for.

The size of the rollers you choose has a direct impact on the sort of shape you create. Whether your hair comes out smooth, wavy, or curly depends on how many times your hair can be wrapped around the roller. Generally speaking, the more times your hair can be wound around the roller, the curlier it will be in the end. Of course, the length of your hair plays a big part in this (as is the type of roller set you go for, but I'll talk more about this as we move forward). If you have extralong hair, you can wrap your hair around even big rollers multiple times, which results in some distinctive curls. Small rollers usually make long hair way too curly because the hair wraps around the roller too many times. On the other hand, if you have shorter hair, you may not even be able to get your hair around a big roller, making small rollers the perfect (and only) option for you. Even if your hair can make only one complete turn around a small roller, you still get noticeably more wave and fullness.

So to determine the right roller size for you, first decide which shape you're going for and then take a clump of your hair and see how many times it wraps around a roller. If you want

wavy hair and your hair wraps one and a half times around a medium-sized roller, then you know that's the right size for you. If you want your hair to be supercurly but you have only chin-length locks, then you likely need to go for petite or small rollers. Take some time to wind rollers through your hair (if the salesperson will let you) or even measure the length of your hair if you need to. As I said, the size of the rollers you choose has a big impact on the type of shapes you can create, so you don't want to end up with the wrong ones!

As a good guide, salon professionals look at roller-setting in the following way:

- One complete turn of your hair around the roller creates soft, C-shaped movements.

- One to two turns around the roller create awesome waviness and fullness.

- More than two turns around the roller create definitive, shapely curls.

TYPES OF ROLLERS

Now that you have an idea which size rollers you want, the next thing you need to think about is what kind of rollers make the most sense for you. There are three basic kinds, and each has its own tale to tell. Let's take a look.

Sponge rollers are soft and comfortable. This makes them the best choice when you plan to leave the rollers in your hair for an extended period of time, for a wet set. You put the rollers into wet hair and allow it to dry, either naturally or, if you're short on time, with the aid of a blow-dryer and/or diffuser. This results in long-lasting and—if you wish—more radical changes in your

> For the strongest possible set you can get with a blow-dryer, after you put all the rollers in place, simply use the diffuser attachment.

style. You truly can get awesome, style-defining curliness in even the straightest natural hair types. Because sponge rollers are soft and supple, you need to fasten them onto your hair with hair clips.

Velcro rollers are generally used only on dry hair because the Velcro tends to snag on wet hair and pull it out of place. On the upside, the Velcro grips dry hair well so no clipping is necessary to secure the roller into place. These rollers let you make quick changes to your shape and style, with two typical uses: Put them in dry hair for five to fifteen minutes to get a wonderful extra kick of body and bounce, or place them in dry hair that you've misted liberally with a blow-dry setting spray or similar setting product and then blast with hot air using the diffuser attachment on your dryer, for a beautiful soft and wavy set to your hair.

Hot rollers are also used only on dry hair. They're heated electrically and are a great time-saver if you want similar effects to a sponge-roller wet set but don't have the time. The results don't last quite as long as a wet set, and you can't create radical changes, but you still get a great change to the way you look. All you have to do is heat the rollers, apply a thermal protector product to protect your hair from the direct heat, and then put them in until they cool, around twenty minutes. These rollers also need clips, but normally you get the clips as part of the package when you buy the set of hot rollers.

Choose Your Set: Wet, Dry, or Hot

These three types of hair setting all offer you great opportunities to temporarily change the natural tendencies of your hair and, more significantly, they let you change and adapt your style, and make any occasion special. All three techniques can be used on any size rollers. The thing to remember is that the type of set you choose influences how soft or firm, and how long-lasting, your set is.

The wet set. Anything you do to your hair when it's still wet and allowed to dry naturally gives you a firmer shape that lasts longer. With the wet set, you place unheated sponge rollers into your wet hair and then let your hair dry naturally—even overnight if you have the time. This gives you your firmest, most lasting set, with a strong and sexy curl or wave (depending on the size of your rollers) that lasts a minimum of three days, probably more, especially if you've let it dry overnight.

You can also blow-dry your hair instead of waiting for it to dry naturally. For the strongest possible set you can get with a blow-dryer, after you put all the rollers in place, simply use the diffuser attachment on your blow-dryer to dry your hair through. You still get great curls or waves with prominent body and bounce, but it's a softer, move movable set that lasts you all day and night, and maybe even the next day, too.

To make sure any set lasts longer, don't pull your hair back into a pony or twist, because that definitely flattens it out. Instead, wear it down, and each morning just go for a quick five-minute blow out with a brush, blow-dryer, and a small amount of a setting or holding product. This revitalizes your waves and curls for a superstylish changed-up do that works for you from day to day.

The dry Velcro roller set. Velcro rollers are put into the hair after you blow-dry. Put a light foam or setting spray into your hair when you come out of the shower and blast it through with a dryer until it is almost, or completely, dry. Now put in a few Velcro rollers for ten to fifteen minutes, hitting them with high heat from the dryer for a minute or so, before letting it cool. This gives you wavy movements, bounce, and

volume, which make your hair easier to work with than if you'd done a wet set (remember, a wet set creates quite firm hold and the hair isn't quite so malleable, at least for the first day or two).

If you haven't got time to wash, blow-dry, and set your hair, a swift fix is to simply mist your dry hair liberally with a setting spray or lotion before putting in Velcro rollers, and blast them all over with heat from your dryer. This gives you a similar, if slightly softer, effect to the traditional way of using Velcro rollers.

The hot roller set. This is my mom's favorite set. Place hot electric rollers into dry hair and then leave them in until they cool, usually around twenty to twenty-five minutes. This type of set is never as firm or long-lasting as the wet set, but the heat still gives your hair lots of marvelous added movement with all the good stuff like waves and curls, body and bounce completely achievable. And again, because your hair is more malleable, you can better manipulate it to create your own hot new style.

How to Set

Whether you choose rollers that are large or small; sponge, Velcro, or electric; or whether you choose a wet, hot, or dry set, the technique for fixing the rollers onto your head is the same—it's called base roller setting. I'll take you through it step by step, and I'll include small amendments for each type of set, which will enable you to get the most out of your roller setting, no matter which method you choose.

1. Depending on the type of set you're going for, your hair will be wet or dry, but either way, begin by gently combing your hair from scalp to ends, preferably with a wide-tooth-comb, to make sure your hair is tangle free and won't snag in the rollers.

2. Next, you need product to make sure your set stays set. The best products for this kind of work include blow-dry setting sprays and lotions, volume-building foams, or anything that works to set your hair long into the night. Now that your hair is tangle-free, apply the product liberally all over your hair. If it's a spray, just mist it all over, making sure to get in at the roots. If it's a foam or crème, work it through from roots to ends. And if you'll be using heat later on, don't forget your thermal protector.

3. It's now time to grab your rollers, and you should certainly sit yourself down in front of a mirror so you can see exactly what you're doing. Don't worry too much about the exact placement of your rollers; just be careful that, whether you're putting in six big rollers or sixteen small ones, you get a nice even spread across the front, top, sides, and back. Do this and your hot new look is sure to be well balanced.

4. Start at the front because that's the easiest place to do it yourself. Part a section of hair that is the same width as the roller, no wider, and give that section another quick comb through to make sure there are no snags. Again, I double-stress that the width of the section of hair you're holding should be the same width as your roller. Why? Because this is the best way to get the consistent curl or wave action that is sure to get you noticed. Pulling hair from outside the width of the roller creates what's called drag. This stops the roller from sitting securely on your head and you end up with less consistent, floppy waves and curls that fail to last.

5. Now that your hair is parted correctly, take that section and pull it up and away from the scalp with your thumb and fingertips. Make sure the hair is taut with no creases or loose bits and hold it in position as close to the tips as you can get without the hair falling free.

6. While holding the section of hair in place, use your free hand to place the roller on the hair as close to the tips of the hair shaft as you can. Wrap the roller

around the hair gently and smoothly, making sure that it catches and holds on to the hair. Now you can place both of your thumbs over the ends of the roller and roll your hair firmly down to the scalp.

7. Once that section is all rolled up, sponge and hot rollers need to be clipped into place. Velcro rollers should hold by themselves, but if you feel more comfortable putting a clip in, that's fine, too.

8. Repeat steps 4–6 with sections all over your head.

9. After all your hair is rolled, apply another liberal amount of setting spray all over your hair, with particular emphasis on the roots of the rolled sections. Note: You need a spray product here because you can't get a foam or crème to reach your roots while the rollers are in place.

10. If you're doing a wet set and want to let it dry naturally for the strongest set, fine. If your hair is long, this can take a couple of hours or more, especially if your hair is also thick. It's a good idea to sleep with these sponge rollers left in, if you can. That way when you wake up you're good to go. Alternatively, you can use a blow-dryer with a diffuser attachment to dry the hair more quickly, but bear in mind that this will affect the firmness and longevity of your set. If you're doing a hot roller set, you need wait only until the rollers are cool before taking them out. For a Velcro dry set, remember that you have already blow-dried your hair before the roller application, so just leave the rollers in for ten to twenty minutes. The longer you leave them in, the more of that gorgeous modern swing and movement you get, but more than twenty minutes is superfluous.

11. When the rollers are ready to come out, unroll and unwind them the same way you put them in—gently and smoothly. Resist any temptation to speed up the process by dragging them out—this definitely destroys your style.

12. Remember, no hairstyle is truly set until it's cool, so give your hair a quick blast of cool air with your dryer. If the style you created is curlier than you wished for, no problem. Just use a blow-dryer and a brush to brush out the curl until you've got the look you want.

13. With a wet set, the slower setting time can give you set lines, a darker band of color running across the line of your hair, at exactly the place where the rollers were placed. Not to worry. For a quick and simple quick fix, brush them out.

14. Now use your fingers or a brush to work your hair into the pattern of your desired style, and be sure to make yourself look stunning. Fix the look into place with a hair or holding spray.

15. If you wish, you can use a straightening or curling iron on the ends to create a custom-made finish to your look. Just curl or twist up any loose ends around the front and sides to add a touch of individual polished elegance. Refine the style with an iron once it's set, rather than trying to create all the shape and texture at once.

The Toolbox

Getting a great change to your hairstyle requires using the right technique with the right products and tools. To make sure you've got the right gear, here's your go-to-guide.

Rollers. You need sponge, Velcro, or hot rollers at your disposal. Think about the types of waves or curls you want to create, because this determines which rollers you want and which size they should be. If you have a few different sizes and types on hand, you significantly expand your styling options.

Clips. Clips are essential to pin sponge or hot rollers into place and can be helpful for Velcro rollers, too.

Product. If you use hot rollers, you need a thermal protector, and everybody needs a good blow-dry setting spray or lotion to set the new look. Hair spray or holding spray is another essential to hold your finished look in place.

Blow-dryer/diffuser. You can dry your wet-set hair with a dryer, but this increases the chance of the rollers getting blown out of position. It's far better to use a diffuser attachment—you get the heat but without the airflow that knocks your rollers and your look out of place.

Hot irons. If you want to tousle up, twist out, or smooth through your finished look, use a straightening or curling iron to add the final touches.

Wide-tooth comb. It's vital that your hair is tangle free so the rollers don't snag. The best way to ensure smoothness is to comb it out gently with a wide-tooth comb.

Quick-Set Options

Now you know how to reset your hair into different wave and curl formations. But what about those days and nights when you'd like to add a bit more glitz and glamour but perhaps don't have the time or inclination to go for a full roller set? Hot irons are your number one solution. Modern hot tools have the power to straighten and smooth, as well as to create curls and movement without the need for rollers. The change isn't as big or dramatic, and it really lasts only through one full day and night before looking a bit limp, but it can still add a special change to your look.

THE CURLING IRON SET

Let's go through it step by step.

1. If your hair is straight to wavy, this is your best bet for a quick transformation. You can use this tool on wet or dry hair, but always apply a thermal protector before you start.

2. Now apply a setting spray, lotion, or foam to aid the strength and longevity of the set.

3. The basics of using this tool are explained in Chapter 5, "Styling at Home," so you should already be well versed in the fundamentals, but also keep in the forefront of your mind that where and how you use your curling iron has a big effect on the looks you can create.

4. If you've got straightish hair and want some nice soft curls and added volume, focus your curling iron application at the roots. This way you get the most volume and lift, enhanced with lovely luscious waves springing out through roots to ends. Repeat all across the front, sides, top, and back for full voluminous curls.

5. If you'd rather go for a tousled look with soft, romantic curly ends to add more femininity to your style, focus your curling iron on the last few inches of your hair shaft instead.

6. Depending on how much curl you desire, you can wrap the iron from the roots halfway up your hair shaft (step 4), or just curl the ends under (step 5). Both looks are easy to achieve—keep experimenting until you find the perfect curling iron set for you. You may even find that a combination of these techniques works great for your style. You can try the more volumized curls (step 4) through the top and back to give you body and bounce combined with some soft, tousled waves (step 5) in the bangs and around the front, adding a polished touch of vintage glamour.

7. Your options don't end there. You can turn your iron under (in toward you and

your scalp) or over (out and away from you and your scalp). Turning the curling iron under brings your curls in toward your head for a polished and feminine finish, while turning the iron out makes your curls roll outward in a more playful, flirty, 1970s look. Both are great, and I encourage you to try them both.

8. Finish by misting hair or holding spray all over to hold and set your look. And if you fancy a touch of dazzle, a few drops of a shine-enhancing product add glamour and glitz.

THE STRAIGHTENING IRON SET

If your hair is naturally curly, but you would like your curls to be set into softer flowing waves but without roller-setting, the tool for you is a straightening iron.

1. Straightening can be done only on dry hair with product being your first port of call. A thermal protector and a setting spray, lotion, or crème should top your list. Apply the thermal protector first, followed by the setting product, which you should apply liberally from roots to ends.

2. The actual styling is oh so easy. Work the iron through sections of your hair nice and straight. Once your hair is straight enough in the front, top, sides, and back, you can play with different styles by gently twisting, rolling, and turning the iron through the final few inches of your hair shaft to create tousled-out midsections and ends.

3. Now, just as with the curling iron set (step 7), if you want to use a straightening iron to curl your ends inward and under, make that motion with your iron, and if you want your curls to swing outward, just twist your iron outward. Easy.

4. Smaller 1" to 1½" straightening irons are better for this kind of manipulation because you can work on smaller sections, which gives you more control.

5. Finish by misting hair or holding spray all over to hold and set your look. If you fancy a touch of dazzle, add a few drops of a shine-enhancing product.

Updo Styling

An updo is defined as any style that involves putting up all or most of your hair. There are two basic ways to do this: the ponytail and the twist. You may remember that it is easier to put curly hair up. When you grab a section and pull it back into a pony, a lot of hair comes with it. That's because, as you pull the hair back, curls lock and grab on to their neighbors, pulling together much more efficiently than straight hair, which isn't rounded and doesn't naturally lock together.

When you pull straight hair back, a lot of hair tends to fall by the wayside. But if you've got straight hair and first make it curly with rollers or an iron, then you get the same benefits as natural curly heads. Another benefit: It's easier to put pins in curly hair because they hook and grab around that textured hair, holding it perfectly in place. In straight hair, pins are more prone to falling out. Not only that, but it's easier to hide the pins in curls. And come on, ladies, what's sexier than a pulled-back pony or twist that has shapely curls or movement to it—so feminine, so foxy?

So anytime you're planning to put your hair up, think about first using a few rollers, or working an iron to create some movement. Then you have a stable foundation for your updo. As you already know from Chapter 5 how to shape ponytails and twists, use this added texture to make your updo styling easier, more creative, successful and, most important, sexy!

The best way to be ready for your special occasion updo is to practice, practice, practice. Put your foundation in, then use a few bands, big pins, grips, or clips to pull your hair up into the sort of shapes you want. Look in the mirror to see how it works for you. You can experiment with different types of dramatic high ponytails, sophisticated low ponytails, and fashion-forward ponytails that sit off center. Try your own versions of the classic twist, too: For a trial run, just take a couple of big pins to hold your hair in place, see if you like the shape, and if and when you do, secure it with a few more big pins to hold the structure. Finally, use smaller pins to hold in the fine details of your newfound special occasion twist.

PONY VARIATIONS

The ponytail is a simple way for any woman to change her day-to-day style. You can use a simple loose and low ponytail when you want to look casual, and you can use a high, more dramatic ponytail when you want to look dressy or dramatic. And once you're comfortable with your basic ponytail (as demonstrated on page 119), there are a whole host of options to give you more variety.

Pin Perfect

The best updos use the fewest pins, so keep it simple, efficient, and direct. Practice getting to grips with the basics—one main anchor and no more than three or four detailing clips, and don't worry about hiding all grips and clips. If the shape is nice, just allow it to look natural and organic.

The quality of grips and clips is important. If a bobby pin doesn't return to its aligned position after use, it's soft and weak, which makes it harder for you to achieve success. Instead, look for professional pins that have a matte or textured finish; these enable greater grip for your styling. Finally, make sure that all pins retain their covered tip edges so they don't snap your hair strands. Holding pins in your mouth is a classic mistake, causing the tip to fail.

Consider bangs. There are two great options that work well with a ponytail. First, you can slick your bangs back so it looks like you don't have any bangs at all. Just use some hairspray (as much as you need) to push and slick your bangs back, making them a part of your ponytail. This gives you a very dramatic and sleeked-back style.

Second, for a softer shape that frames your eyes, simply comb your bangs into a side part, pushing your bangs to the side of your face. It's a modern and sexy way to complement any ponytail.

Next, I recommend trying something even simpler: Drape a few pieces of your ponytail loosely around your neck. Once your ponytail is in place, gently drag out a few pieces of tied-back hair and let them fall naturally. Don't make them look too perfect; let them appear loose, casual, and messy. Loosely draped and free hair strands are all at once playful, sensual, and refined, and it's so easy you have to try it.

The emboldened at-home hairdoer can try the side ponytail, placing it at the side of your head rather than in the back. When you look in the mirror, you see your pony draped over one side of your face, hanging over your ear. It's exactly the same technique as with the basic ponytail; just make sure to create a side part on the opposite side of your pony, as this gives the look a better overall balance. This is great if your hair has natural curl and movement; the side pony appears much gentler and more forgiving, that way. This is a bold high-fashion statement, so be sure that's the statement you want to make before you wear it out.

Finally, here's something every woman should try. Put some curl and movement into your hair and then place it into a sophisticated high ponytail. This is a beautiful look that creates lots of looseness, lots of free texture, and it's soft and feminine. Simply create some curly textural waves in the back of your hair by following the techniques in either sections on the creating curl or curling irons, pages 114 and 226 (of course, if you're lucky enough to have naturally curly hair you don't have to worry about this!), then place those curly waves into the top of your high ponytail. Again, you are creating your ponytail by using the basic ponytail technique, but now your hair has curl and movement. Once your pony is set in place, you can use fine hairpins to pin the curls to the back of your head, helping them sit flat and hold their shape all day, all night.

Special Days

Now that you've mastered roller-setting and have some classic updos in your style locker, you can tailor your styling to all kinds of special occasions.

One big piece of advice before you embark on all this change: Try out your do first. The last thing you want is to spend the money and the time to *look* fabulous but not *feel* fabulous. One client came to me the morning of her daughter's wedding. Sheila had already had the makeup artist come to her house and do a full "wedding" face, appropriate for a mother of the bride. She looked quite glamorous, but it was more than I was used to seeing on her.

We had discussed her wedding hair. She had looked beautiful, very glamorous and elegant, but very done, like an old-time movie star.

Sheila was due back for her usual cut about a month later. The minute she planted herself in my chair, I asked about the wedding and how she felt about her look.

I was devastated by the woeful expression on her face.

"It was awful," she said.

"It was your daughter's wedding. How could that be awful?"

"I just didn't feel like myself." Sheila explained that although everyone told her how beautiful she looked, she just didn't feel like herself. After the pictures were taken, she went into the bathroom, took off half her makeup, and loosened the chignon into a more casual style. "It wasn't perfect," she said, "but it felt more me. Then I had a great time."

Lesson learned. Try out the whole look—hair, makeup, everything—at least once before your big occasion.

I'm all for change and don't think people should always just stick with what feels comfortable, but you need to revel in that change and not want to hide. If Sheila

> **T**ry out your do first. The last thing you want is to spend the money and the time to *look* fabulous but not *feel* fabulous.

decided on a low, elegant chignon. After seeing that full face of makeup, I asked if she was sure. I thought perhaps she would feel too stark and severe. But this was what she had had in her mind for the last year, so chignon it was. She had known before how she would feel, she probably would have done less makeup or softer hair.

Here are my top picks for six special occasions.

NIGHT OUT WITH THE GIRLS

What a great time to have fun with your hair! For this type of occasion I love styles that look natural and casual—nothing too forced. Think about making your hair look flirty and fashionable because, for me, that's always a winner, especially when you can talk about how you created such a wonderful yet casual do with all your friends! Anything that bounces with kicks and flicks is an awesome head turner. And make sure you get a few pieces of hair to fall and drape around your face, especially if you can use an iron to put some understated wave movements into it—utterly fabulous. Set your hair so it has movement and softness. Go for a style that is cute and sexy. As I said before, I get a big kick out of seeing cascading waves that have been pulled back into a sophisticated low-slung or off-to-the-side pony. So why not try roller-setting with big rollers to give you that gushing, tumbling, waterfall effect? Then, all you have to do is create that low pony and you, and your look, will be the envy of all your friends.

DATE NIGHT

You want to look stunning but not over the top. More than anything, give your hairstyle sex appeal. If you're a curly, go for a wet set and set your hair into smooth and sleek romantic waviness. If you have unruly flyaway hair, pull it away from your face into a classic pony or twist—that way you won't be thinking about it throughout the night. Whenever I'm styling a woman's hair for her date night, I definitely want to make her look classy and polished and pulled together; that should be your aim, too. But you don't want hair that you—and your man!—can't run your fingers through. That's no good if you get a kiss and a cuddle, because men like to touch and caress hair. Go for something stylish, special, and different, but easy to wear and easy to touch. You don't want anything too elaborate and nothing that needs a bagful of pins to hold it up. Maybe finish your look with a high shine product to give your hair a healthy, sexy glow. It's worth taking the time to make yourself look great, and you'll feel fabulous.

OFFICE PARTY

Office parties tend to begin at clocking-off time, so you want something that is a quick change from your day-to-day hair and adds a bit more drama to your look—sternly professional no more, ready to party for sure. Stick a hot iron (either a curling iron or straightening iron) and setting or holding spray in your bag so you can go for that swift fix. You can go through the hair section by section, lifting your hair up at the root, misting in the product, and then using the iron to create extra smoothness or some wave and curl movements—whatever works for you.

Even changing the position of your part gives you an instant change, or for more distinction, clip your hair off to the side. And don't forget about the ponytail. Ponies are super easy to do and, for this occasion, I love the high pony. It says, "Hey, I'm modern and fun, and look at all the wonderful movement in my hair." You get lift, drama, and not just a little polished elegance, thereby hitting your work colleagues with a sudden and striking surprise. If your office party is in the holiday season, you can think about adding more glitz to your look. Accessorize with a high-sparkle (fake!) diamond barrette, or if that's too much for you, holiday-inspired clips and grips are a great option, making you look seasonal.

WEDDING

On your most special day, your hairstyle, simply *has* to last. Because of this, consider getting your hair styled professionally. You want to look absolutely sensational, timeless (you'll be looking at your wedding photos for a long time!), and coordinated with your dress and the theme of your day, and the best way to piece all of those things together is to go to a professional.

So let's talk about the professional wedding-day do. It's imperative you go for a consultation first, as this gives you the chance to try out your ideas and see if you like the results. Before you go to your appointment, think about what you'd like to achieve. It's a great idea to take inspiration from the theme of your day. Is your day simple or elaborate? Does it reflect a certain era—the 1920s or 1940s, for example? Is it a modern-day casual beach wedding? Remember, too, that the simplest wedding styles, the ones that are whimsical and flattering, are generally considered the best. If you do want something elaborate and ornamental, fine, but make it that way in the back, rather than in the front—just as wedding dresses are uncomplicated in the front and feature decoration in the back. There's no need to overcomplicate the front because the focus should be on you and your natural beauty, not on your hair.

Consider these things when thinking about your hairdo, then find some pictures of hair that you like in bridal magazines. Go to your consultation armed with a good selection of pictures and a good selection of ideas. Take a digital camera with you to take pictures of the stylist's work and then ask him or her to vary it a little. Wedding consultations aren't cheap, so you may as well make your stylist earn his or her keep. Don't worry, if you don't like the first creation, that's why you've gone in advance and not left it until your special day! Once you've worked with your hairdresser to find the right shape and style for you, don't expect your wedding day do to be an exact match to the consultation version. It should be 90 or 95 percent the same, but always allow for little differences.

If you are doing your wedding hairdo at

home, keep it supersimple. Practice it over and over again with your maid of honor. On the big day, give yourself plenty of time, make it easy to manage, and you definitely want hairspray to fix the hair away from your face. The simplest piece of decoration could really make your look; one well-placed flower adds rich ornate beauty to your style. Go for something simple, elegant, and timeless.

If you're a bridesmaid, make sure that your style matches that of the bride, but don't upstage her—that's bad wedding etiquette. Check in with her to see what style she's going for and style your hair to be a subtle variation on that theme, but nothing overpowering.

VACATION

When you're on vacation, you don't want to carry lots of tools with you. It's too much hassle, and, besides, lots of heat tool work causes more damage to your hair when you combine it with the damage caused by the sun and ocean. Instead, take the casual, natural, and healthy approach. Look to give your hair a nice glow, and if you want a style that goes from day to night, then use product to create a nice, natural shape. This is a great time to accessorize: Go for simple low ponytails with a hat or a scarf, which make you look beach-savvy, with the added benefit of protecting your hair from the sun.

JOB INTERVIEW

The key element on a job interview is to look professional, polished, and well groomed. Make sure you've got a great haircut, and, if you're into color, there should be no roots showing. You'll most likely be sitting across a desk from your interviewer, so it's the top half of you that he or she will be looking at and connecting with. Keep your hair out of your face so you don't have to keep pushing it out of your eyes. Whenever I conduct an interview with a potential employee, I always look for him or her to be wearing a hair shape and a style befitting a modern pulled-together professional, and a similar approach is definitely your best bet. Don't go for a style that you would never normally try to do. I've seen it myself—people come in for an interview looking great, and then on their first day they look totally different. Make sure to style your hair in a way that, if they ask you back, still looks like you when you return.

When You're Out and About and Your Flashy Look Flops

You spent all that time creating a gorgeous and sexy special-occasion do. You shaped wonderful waves or cascading curls and now, when you're out and about, and you're catching the eye for such a fabulous style-enhancing change, your hair begins to droop. The curls are falling flat, the waves have wilted. What can you do?

First of all, don't panic. This happens to everyone at one time or another—I've even seen some of my very own stylists dashing off to the ladies' room to fix a drooping hairdo during a big night out in the city. Realizing your hair has gone bad is more than half the battle. You know it's happened if the fullness and volume, so apparent in roller setting, have gone. Your waves or curls are no longer bouncy and voluptuous, more deflated and dull. Being able to pick up the pieces from a special style gone wrong in the middle of an occasion is a requirement for the modern style-conscious woman.

As I say, this can happen to anyone. The humidity or, if you're inside, the air-conditioning or proximity of bodies (and consequently hot air) may well have caused the droop, so don't beat yourself up. Preparation is the key—have tools on hand that can fix your flopping do. Always carry in your bag a mid- to firm-hold hair or holding spray and a few pins, grips, and clips. Whisk yourself off to powder your nose and now you can use your holding spray. Mist it in all over and then use your fingers to gently push your hair up into its former style. Holding sprays are designed to build structure and defeat droopiness, helping you revitalize your look with lift, shine, and polish. But don't stop there—if it's fallen once, it can fall again. Take your pins, grips, or clips and pull your hair back or set it to the side, pin it in place, give it a final mist of holding spray, and you're good to go. You might even take this chance to pull out a few loose strands of hair around the front and let them drape and frame your face. And if your friends or date ask you what happened, just say, "What, oh my hair? Nothing. I just fancied a change!"

Summing It All Up

My final chapter of *Great Hair* encourages you to take all your newfound knowledge about hair care and hair styling and go one step further by creating magical special-occasion hair.

The trick is to build a foundation for your new special style by setting your hair into waves and curls that are full of body and bounce. There are a couple of ways to do this. First, you can set your hair with rollers. Remember that different sizes and different types do different things. Use a bigger roller for smooth and wavy looks; use a smaller roller for curlier hair. Sponge rollers can be left in the hair the longest and consequently have the biggest potential to create the most radical and lasting changes in your hairstyle. Velcro rollers should be left in the hair for only fifteen or twenty minutes and create soft waves with lots of body and bounce. Hot rollers should be left in the hair until it is cool (around twenty minutes) and also create lots of movement and bounce with waves and soft curls completely achievable.

For a quicker solution, use my quick-set options that utilize the curling iron and straightening iron for quicker, if less lasting, changes. They're a great option for a speedy, fantastic change.

When you want to put your hair up into a foxy and feminine style, use my updo styling section and guidelines on pony variations and pins to create the look you want.

I finish the chapter with some ideas for styles that will suit the special days in your life. Have fun creating them and have even more fun wearing them!

A Final Word from Nick

After more than twenty-five years in the hairdressing industry as a stylist, mentor, and educator, I am truly amazed by and still in awe of the power we have with our craft. All of us at Arrojo Studio receive many letters of thanks for the positive impact of the haircuts and colors we've created. These hairstyles change the way people look and feel, and because of that, they change people's lives as well.

"Look great, feel fabulous" is the tagline I use to encourage all people to change, to try something new and reinvigorating. My hope—and the inspiration for writing *Great Hair* in the first place—is that this book will encourage you to love your hair as something you have been blessed with, something you can constantly change, and something you can have a lot of fun with—whether getting a new cut, a new color, styling your hair from day to day, or styling your hair for a special occasion.

My technique is to work with the hair rather than against it. My motivation is to empower all clients (and stylists, too!) with knowledge. My purpose is to inspire a fresh perspective of newness and vitality, but also impart realism about what each person's hair can achieve. Throughout this book I never tried to create the impossible and unrealistic but, rather, worked *with* the hair, the features, the physique, and the personality to get the right look for each individual. Look your

best, not somebody else's best. That's the easiest approach for a successful hairstyle. It's the way I tackle every single haircut and it's the way—whether you are thinking about a cut, a color, or your day-to-day styling—you should approach your hair, too.

If I were to see the clients in this book again in five years' time, with a different perspective and a different sense of fashion and style, I am convinced most of the hair styles would be different. And this is key for all the readers of my book: Times change, so learn to adapt for a fresh and modern style.

I've also learned from this wonderful experience. While working on the makeover and style guide sections, we revamped so many different women, all for the better. We made so many people happy. Not just with the way that they looked, but with the way they felt as well. The overriding excitement of change was a fantastic firsthand experience. The opportunity to see spirits lifted, the sharing of that moment when our models realized how beautiful they really are. Husbands and fathers seeing their loved ones feel this excitement, this joy of beauty. It drives home how important hair is to us all.

All of our models are real people, and many traveled from far and wide to experience a new style. Some changes were dramatic; some were subtle. But for all, as I always say, it's not what's come off, it's what's kept on. For those who lost more than ten inches of hair, we sent the trimmed-off tresses to Locks of Love. Such a great cause and a fantastic benefit to the experience of change that these women felt.

See a visit to your stylist as a chance to be pampered and cared for. It's a time to relax and smile, to be completely refreshed. I encourage you all to seek out someone you trust, believe in, and can enjoy. A great style makes you look and feel youthful and beautiful. Please keep an open mind and don't close the door or give up if you cannot immediately find your special stylist. I know from my work up and down the country that there are lots of great hairdressers, and if you remain open to change and commit to finding the right one for you, then a great style will never be far away.

As long as I'm working, I will continue to teach, encourage, and mentor other hair-dressers to raise standards in the craft that I love. This book, though, is meant to educate you, the client who sits in our chair. It gives you a greater sense of power, understanding, and knowledge about your own hair. But don't be surprised if you see this book on the table of your local salon's reception area, because I'm sure that stylists, young and old, will enjoy this book as well. They may even be able to use it to help get a better understanding of their clients, to show them some new hairstyles they may like, and to talk through styling techniques that they can use at home each day.

Now that you have all of my knowledge, use it to understand and care for your own unique hair. Use it to find some styles you love and want to wear. Use it to discover your own great stylist. Use it to enjoy successful styling at home each and every day. Use it to get great hair color that brightens up your best features. Use it to turn problem hair into perfect hair. Use it to style your

ethnic hair. Use it to give you that Wow! factor on any kind of special day. More than anything, use it as the inspiration to help you enjoy changing your looks and keep your perspective about hair and style fresh.

Finally, the most joy that this book gave me was seeing many of the models coming back into my salon a few months after the photo shoot to see another stylist and get a new, different look. Or, for those who lived farther away, the letters of thanks that let me know how special they felt and how the experience had taught them always to keep their hair current and contemporary. These women experienced beautiful newness in all its sprightly and youthful glory. It inspired them to keep changing, to keep trying fun new looks, and to use hair as an accessory to their own personal style—an accessory that can change, inspire, and revitalize. That brought unbridled joy to me because that's exactly the approach that will keep them—and you—looking great and feeling fabulous. To have any part in inspiring those thoughts is an honor and a privilege.

Look through the pictures of me in this book and you'll see that my hair changes, too! I don't want to keep the same style forever, nor should you. Change is good.

Glossary

Here's a list of the tools, products, and techniques I talk about in the book. I give a brief explanation of each so that you have a quick reference guide on hand whenever you need it. I also include short explanations for a few terms and phrases that may not be immediately recognizable to some.

bangs. The part of your hair that drapes over and across your forehead and eyes, framing the features of your face. Very sexy!

blow-dry setting spray. A styling product that prepares the hair for a beautiful, full blow-dry.

blow-dryer. Tool that blows hot (and cold) air to straighten, curl, shape, and style your hair. An essential product for all.

blow out. Refers to the blow-dry, as in, "What a great blow out."

bobby pin. A small metal hairpin used to hold the hair in place.

buildup and residue. When you shampoo and fail to rinse thoroughly, the result is shampoo suds sitting on the scalp, causing irritation and flakiness. Buildup and residue also result if you use lots of styling product and don't shampoo regularly, giving you oily, greasy hair.

bungee band. A versatile elastic hair band that locks the hair into place using hooks at each end of the elastic.

conditioner. Product that gives hair extra moisture, shine, softness, and manageability. Essential for healthy-looking and lustrous hair.

cool-shot button. Hit this button on your blow-dryer for a blast of cool air to fix and set your look into place.

cornrows. Small fine rows of hair braided tightly to the scalp to produce a pattern.

cup and scrunch. A styling technique used for curly hair that isn't being blown dry or diffused. It literally means cupping and scrunching all your curls with your hands (from when the hair is wet until it is almost dry, at regular intervals) to get beautiful, bouncy curly hair.

curl crème. A styling product tailored to—and essential for—curly hair. Activates curls while fighting the frizz that is common with this hair type.

curling iron. A heat-based hair-styling tool used for creating waves and curls in straighter hair types.

cuticle. The outer layer of your hair shaft, the bit you see.

deep conditioner. Similar to regular conditioner products but full of a feast of proteins, vitamins, and nutrients to restore vitality in under-nourished, chemically treated, and chronically dry hair. Should be used only once a week at most.

defrizz serum. A styling product that controls flyaways, eases excess volume, and eliminates frizz. Can be used on straight and curly hair types.

demipermanent color. Mild color that adds luster and depth, freshens permanent colors, and changes tone.

density. The amount of hairs on your head. If you have loads of hair, your hair has heavy density; if you have less hair, your hair has light density.

diffuser. A styling tool for curly hair types. The air of a blow-dryer blows curls out of place, resulting in a loss of style. A diffuser attached to the dryer diffuses this airflow, while retaining the heat, so you can dry your curly hair quickly and easily without disturbing curls.

extensions. Human or artificial external lengths of hair that can be tracked, woven, glued, or braided into your hair for extra length. See *weave* and *weft.*

flyaways. Cheeky little pieces of hair that like to "fly away" from the rest of your style, sticking up and destroying your look. Use a hair, holding, or shine spray to flatten them out.

frizz. Hair that is dry and porous is usually frizzy. Frizz occurs at the ends of the hair shaft, and that part of the hair tends to "frizz" away from the rest of the style, creating an unhealthy-looking finish. Cutting off the damaged ends is the only surefire way to get rid of frizz, but using moisture-rich shampoos and conditioners and frizz-fighting styling products helps.

graduation. A cutting technique in which there is a subtle and gradual buildup of weight, typically in the back of the hair, that adds strength and style to many different looks.

hair crème. A modern, light-hold styling product that is rich in moisture, to give you a smooth, natural-looking, and sexy style.

hair gel. A classic firm-hold styling product to slick, set, and shape all hairstyles.

hairnet. A small, often elasticized, fine net worn over long hair to hold it in place, particularly when you are roller-setting your hair overnight.

hairpin. A long metal tool used to hold hair in place.

hair shaft. The full length of one piece of hair, from root to end.

heat stress. Damage to your hair caused by using a lot of heat tools (blow-dryers, straightening irons, flat irons) consistently over a period of time.

highlights. Lighter color that provides variation in hair tone. There are face-framing highlights, half-head highlights, and full-head highlights. Compare *lowlights.*

holding spray. A styling product that gives long-lasting hold and control to all hair types.

ionic technology. A recent technical innovation that is used in blow-dryers, brushes, and straightening and curling irons to add extra shine, smoothness, and strength, and reduce static and frizz in medium to thick and chemically treated hair.

keratin. A fibrous protein forming the main structural constituent of healthy hair. It can also be found in deep conditioners because dry and damaged hair has typically lost a lot of keratin and deep conditioners restore that lost health.

large round brush. A styling tool used to add lots of volume, or to create big loose waves.

layers. A classic hairdressing technique that removes weight and bulkiness by cutting much shorter pieces that fall above your desired length.

leave-in conditioner. Lightweight and daily conditioners, and indeed conditioners labeled "leave-in" or something similar, can be left in the hair rather than rinsed out. They add extra moisture, shine, and smoothness, and also make hair more manageable.

level system. A system used by hair colorists to value the natural level of lightness or darkness in your hair color. It ranges from black to lightest blond and helps the colorist establish what hair colors are most suitable for you.

lowlights. The same as highlights, but providing darker rather than lighter tones.

medium round brush. A styling tool that adds lift and volume, and creates soft waves and curls.

mousse. A classic styling product that holds, controls, and lifts.

natural wet set. The cupping and scrunching technique is often labeled the "natural wet set," as you set your curls into place naturally.

nozzle. An essential attachment to your blow-dryer that focuses the heat where you want it to go for a more controlled blow-dry.

one-length line. Rather than cutting in layers or texturizing the interior, all the hair reaches the same length, providing a strong, solid structure.

permanent color. Strong, dynamic color in a complete range of tones.

pieciness. A hairdresser's word to describe short and heavily textured haircuts that have a lot of separation in the length, making the style look choppy and messy.

pigment. Your natural hair color. Everybody has either more red pigment or more yellow pigment in her hair. The more red pigment, the darker your natural hue; the more yellow pigment, the lighter your natural hue.

porosity. The hair's ability to absorb and retain moisture. Hair that doesn't retain moisture has a lot of porosity. Porous hair is extradry and normally full of frizz. Hair that has been through too much heat-tool styling or chemical treatments is most prone to being porous. It doesn't look healthy.

razor cut. Any haircut that is done with a razor rather than scissors.

rollers. Styling tools that you wrap your hair around, leaving the rollers in the hair for a short or extended time to create more wave, curl, and movement in your style. Rollers come in three types: sponge, Velcro, and hot.

roller-set. Using rollers to give yourself a set style.

scissor cut. Any haircut that is done with scissors.

semipermanent color. Temporary hair color (lasting no more than twelve shampoos). Adds shine, fullness, and depth in a variety of subtle tones.

shampoo. A product that cleanses your hair. Has lots of suds and lather, and a good one leaves your hair clean, refreshed, and smelling lovely.

shine spray. A styling product that shines up your style, giving you more glitz and dazzle. Most shine sprays also fight flyaways and leave your hair flat and smooth.

small round brush. A styling tool best used on short hairstyles. Great for adding lift, smoothness, and volume. Can also be wrapped around the hair to create curly ringlets.

split ends. The tips of hair that have split open, making it impossible to achieve a successful style. Causes include dryness, too much heat-tool styling, or too many chemical treatments—and not enough care to restore the moisture. The only guaranteed way to get rid of them is to cut them off.

straightening iron. A heat-based styling tool used to press your hair smooth, straight, and flat.

styling crème. A product that builds volume with lots of hold. Great for when you want to roller-set your hair.

swing and movement. Describes a cut that creates space in your hair so that it moves freely and sexily.

taking the weight out. A cutting technique for thick and bulky hair. Your stylist cuts into the interior of your hairstyle to remove those bulky and unnecessary pieces that can weigh down your look.

temperature gauge. Good hot tools have a temperature gauge so you can see exactly how much heat you are applying to your hair.

texture paste. A styling product that creates pieciness, separation, and loose and messy textures in short to midlength styles.

texturizing. Removes weight or bulk in your hair to provide a lighter look with lots of movement and fluidity.

thermal reconditioning. Permanent process that makes thick, dense, and curly ethnic hair straight, smooth, and shiny.

thermal protector. A product that protects your hair from heat damage by providing a barrier against the heat. Essential for anyone using heat tools.

tourmaline. The key ingredient in ionic technology, tourmaline is a semiprecious crystal and natural source of the ion energy that makes hair styling in medium to thick hair, and in chemically treated hair, more effective.

track. When you want to put an extra hairpiece into your hair, it's essential to create a "track" that the extended hair piece can be sewn in to. This track—or hem—works like an anchor to hold the new hair in place.

undercutting. Cutting hair underneath shorter than top layers. Makes cut livelier and fuller and gives the illusion of body and bounce.

vent brush. The air goes through the vents in the brush as you blow-dry, allowing for faster, more effective styling in short to midlength hairstyles.

virgin head. Anyone who has never had any hair color or other chemical treatment service performed on her hair.

volume foam. A styling product best used to lift up, thicken, volumize, and support all hairstyles. An essential product for fine, limp, and lifeless hair.

weave. A separate hairpiece sewn or glued along a "track" to add length and/or color.

weft. Loose strands of synthetic hair braided into your natural hair to add length and/or color.

wet set. Rollers put into wet hair and left in for an extended period of time—even overnight—to create the longest-lasting kind of roller-set.

wide-tooth comb. A great styling aid for all hair types, but especially curly textures. Use it to comb hair after applying styling product for even distribution.

Arrojo Studio and Products

Arrojo Studio is located in lower Manhattan. You are welcome to come visit us to check out the studio and see the great styles, cuts, and colors we are giving our clients. Or call to make an appointment for a free consultation.

All Arrojo products are available at the studio: shampoos, conditioners, style and finishing products, tools, travel packs, gift packs, cool T-shirts, and much more. You can also order products on our Web site. Please visit our snazzy site, where you can get information about our team, services, products, and education.

You deserve Great Hair!

Arrojo Studio
180 Varick Street
New York, N.Y. 10014
212-242-7786
www.arrojostudio.com
www.arrojoeducation.com
www.arrojoproduct.com